The Green Rocket Cookbook

VIBRANT VEGAN RECIPES THAT PUT FLAVOUR FIRST

PHILIP PEARCE

The Green Rocket Cookbook
©2021 Philip Pearce &
Meze Publishing Limited
First edition printed in 2021 in the UK
ISBN: 978-1-910863-86-2
Written by: Philip Pearce
Edited by: Katie Fisher, Phil Turner
Photography by:
Rob Wicks (eatpictures.com)
Designed by: Paul Cocker
PR: Emma Toogood, Lizzy Capps
Contributors: Katherine Dullforce, Lis Ellis
Michael Johnson, Lizzie Morton
Printed and bound in the UK by
Bell & Bain Ltd, Glasgow

Published by Meze Publishing Limited
Unit 1b, 2 Kelham Square
Kelham Riverside
Sheffield S3 8SD
Web: www.mezepublishing.co.uk
Telephone: 0114 275 7709
Email: info@mezepublishing.co.uk

The Green Rocket

Award Winning Ca

akfast, Lunch & I

CONTENTS

RECIPE LIST

ABOUT US

The Green Rocket is a proudly independent and multi-award-winning restaurant in Bath, with vibrant vegan food that puts flavour at its core.

My lifelong dream was always to set up my own café and restaurant. My parents owned food pubs when my sister and I were kids, so I had plenty of early experience... washing dishes graduated to basic food prep, and after leaving school I took various chef jobs in my home city of Bath. My career in the food industry then took me to Australia and New Zealand for ten years, where I worked with some great chefs including Peter Chaplin, who was Madonna's private chef for her world tours, as well as writing recipes for a cookery programme on primetime national television. Travel is a great teacher and I tried to pick up tips and ideas everywhere I went, from accountancy and management to curating wine lists. Learning on the job and seeing the world definitely influenced my cooking, which meant I could expand my repertoire to a wide range of cuisines and styles.

I returned to the UK with the goal of focusing on my own place. It wouldn't have worked to try and open a vegetarian and vegan establishment in New Zealand; Europe was a little further ahead in terms of that food scene. I'd got somewhat bored of fine dining by this point: stuffy dining rooms, foams on everything and cubes of gel felt dull to me and sucked the joy out of eating. So The Green Rocket was going to be somewhere people could come once a week, not once a year having saved up to afford it. The café and restaurant would serve decent meals at fair prices, from breakfast to dinner with good coffee and good wine available. You could walk in, creating an atmosphere that felt informal and full of laughter but not too casual with excellent service that would make everyone feel welcome.

In Bath at that time, The Green Rocket definitely filled a gap between the entry-level places and the excellent Demuths (later Acorn) which was more of a fine dining restaurant. We planted ourselves at the higher end of the middle, and especially wanted to offer great meat-free breakfasts which were difficult to find. We weren't unique in only serving vegan and vegetarian food, but having been a vegetarian myself since the age of 15 (and vegan since 17) I know first-hand that many people following plant-based diets don't feel too comfortable eating in restaurants that serve meat. At The Green Rocket, anybody can eat anything on the menu – dietary restrictions aside, although we do try to cater for gluten-free customers as much as possible – and I feel that we've carved out a space for ourselves according to that ethos.

• **Breakfast**

• **Lunch**

• **Dinner**

More than eight years on from its opening, the café and restaurant still has regulars who come several times a week, or every Sunday morning for breakfast. We get to know faces and some people have been visiting us since the very beginning. It all comes down to one simple element: tasty food. We make our menus interesting, vibrant, fresh and above all delicious. I do think that too many vegetarian establishments go wrong in trying to be everybody's doctor: plant-based food can be healthy, but why wouldn't you put flavour first? Food is about enjoyment and so it has to look and taste the best it can.

I also want everyone to be able to create tasty food themselves and to recognise that 'vegan food' is absolutely not just for vegans. Probably 85% of our customers at The Green Rocket aren't vegetarian or vegan, which goes a long way to proving that plant-based cuisine can be vibrant and delicious. To reflect our menu, many of the recipes in this book are also gluten-free because we want them to be accessible to everyone. Our food is interesting but approachable, and truthfully we have been asked by our customers to create a cookbook since we opened. As unfortunate as the pandemic has been, it gave us that now-or-never window to compile some of our favourite recipes from over the years and share those little bits of technique that elevate restaurant cooking, whether that's salting your pasta water or making a risotto properly as one of my Sicilian chefs taught me.

We pride ourselves on sticking to high standards of presentation and flavour at The Green Rocket, which you can only achieve with great attention to detail. Having said that, I believe that cookbooks should be guides to making something tasty in your own kitchen, so if you do want to change up ingredients here and there, go for it. The chapters over the following pages reflect how we put menus together in the restaurant; I personally love to eat tapas-style meals which have that flexibility, so we offer small and large plates to pick and choose from. Whatever your level of skill and however you normally put a meal together, I hope that these recipes give you the tools to create really tasty food at home. That's what it's all about and what we'll always aim to offer at The Green Rocket. Enjoy.

Philip Pearce, Chef Owner

ACKNOWLEDGEMENTS

A restaurant relies on teamwork, and I am pleased to say that we have an exceptionally skilled team at The Green Rocket: Matt, Gwydion, Bogdan, Jacob, Jake, Amelia, Louise, Mukhia, Imogen and Ellie.

I would like to also give a shout out to some of our previous team members since 2013 who really stick out in my mind. These people went above and beyond, people who you would want next to you in the trenches. They are Jackson, Jye, Cosmin & Rachael (who are now married after meeting at the Green Rocket), George Lunn, Tansy 'Super Tans' Dando, James Gordon, Will Garner and Bartek. Thank you all, you kept the plates spinning.

Other notable mentions who have been a huge help with running the restaurant as well as making this book possible:

Georgia, Matt, Helen and Rachel of Demuths Cookery School.

Tim Coffey from The Real Italian Pizza Company.

My parents, for all their help in a multitude of ways.

Cristy, Amalie and Evie for tolerating all the long hours I do, the mess and recipe testing at home.

My two dogs, Steeps and Twig.

All my suppliers over the years, especially in the early days when we were robbing Peter to pay Paul, many of which we have stayed loyal to since we opened our doors for the first time on the 8th of February 2013.

A big hearty thanks to all our customers over the years. You are the most important part and the reason we do what we do. This recipe book exists because of all your requests to produce one over the last nine years.

Breakfasts

BERRY SMOOTHIE BOWL

Preparation time: 5 minutes
Serves 4
Gluten-free

Use this recipe as a rough guide: change up the berries and nut butters for different flavours. This is a great breakfast because it is so quick, healthy and delicious.

300g mixed berries

3 bananas, peeled

300ml soya milk

150g gluten-free oats

3 tablespoons almond butter

4 tablespoons agave or maple syrup

Granola, to decorate (optional)

Set a few berries aside for decoration, then blend all the ingredients except the granola in a food processor. Leave the mixture slightly coarse for some texture and adjust the sweetness to your preference. Decorate the smoothie bowl with the remaining berries and some granola, if using.

BLOODY MARY TOMATOES

Preparation time: 10 minutes
Cooking time: 10 minutes
Serves 4
Gluten-free when using gluten-free bread

This dish was developed after kitchen discussions about putting a Bloody Mary on our breakfast menu, which unfortunately we couldn't do because our alcohol licence does not start until 10am. So instead, we just reworked the classic cocktail into a meal! Adding vodka is definitely optional though.

Olive oil

2 shallots, sliced

2 sticks of celery, sliced

8 very ripe tomatoes on the vine, quartered

Tabasco, to taste

Vegan Worcestershire sauce

Vodka (optional)

A few sprigs of fresh parsley

Salt and pepper, to taste

Sourdough, to serve

Heat a frying pan, then add a little olive oil, Add the sliced shallots and celery to cook on a low heat until starting to soften. Add the quartered tomatoes and turn up the heat to medium, then cook until soft but not breaking down. If you are using smaller tomatoes, just cut them in half.

Now add some Tabasco, a few shakes of Worcestershire sauce and a little splash of vodka (go on, live a little!) and cook for another minute. Add the parsley, tearing the leaves off any larger stalks, and season the mixture with salt and pepper. Serve the tomatoes on some good, toasted sourdough.

BREAKFAST BAKED BEANS

Preparation time: 15 minutes, plus soaking overnight
Cooking time: 1 hour
Makes enough to fill a 2 litre container
Gluten-free

This recipe makes a large batch so it can be frozen into portions and defrosted when required. I find it difficult to eat baked beans from a tin anymore as they taste awful in comparison! Adjust the sugar/sweetener content to your preference.

300g haricot beans

1/2 teaspoon bicarbonate of soda

Olive oil

1 medium white onion, finely diced

1 stick of celery, finely diced

1 large sprig of thyme

1/2 tablespoon finely chopped fresh rosemary

1 clove of garlic, finely chopped

1 teaspoon paprika

500ml passata

500ml vegetable stock

1 1/2 tablespoons white sugar or agave syrup

Salt and pepper

Soak the haricot beans overnight in a bowl of water with the bicarbonate of soda stirred in. When you're ready to cook, drain the beans and then boil them in a large pan of fresh water (without salt) until almost cooked.

In a separate pan, heat a little oil and gently sauté the diced onion and celery. When they start to soften, add the fresh herbs and garlic to cook for a few minutes. Now add the paprika and cook for another 2 minutes.

Stir in the tomato passata and half of the stock, then cook for a couple of minutes before adding the drained cooked beans and sugar or agave. Cook on a gentle simmer for approximately 45 minutes, adding the remaining stock as required. Cook the beans until they are soft but still hold together; their texture should not be floury.

Taste the baked beans and season with salt and pepper accordingly. This recipe will be a lot less sweet than tinned beans from a supermarket, so adjust the sweetness to your preference.

BREAKFAST ROSTI

Preparation time: 15 minutes
Cooking time: 20 minutes
Serves 4
Gluten-free

This is a great brunch dish to share with friends: crispy potato rosti served with portobello mushrooms, roasted tomatoes, wilted spinach, scrambled tofu and a sweet potato purée for a colourful and delicious start to the day.

1 punnet of ripe cherry tomatoes on the vine

4 portobello mushrooms, cleaned and stalk removed

6 tablespoons olive oil

Salt and pepper

1 sweet potato (optional)

1kg white potatoes (choose a good all-rounder)

300g silken tofu

1 tablespoon nutritional yeast flakes

1 teaspoon black salt

1/4 teaspoon turmeric

100g cooking spinach

Preheat your oven to approximately 180°c degrees and put the tomatoes and mushrooms on a baking tray. Drizzle them with some olive oil and season with salt and pepper. Bake in the preheated oven for approximately 15 minutes or until they start to soften. The mushrooms may need an extra 5 minutes depending on their size.

Meanwhile, if you are making the sweet potato purée, peel and chop the sweet potato then cook in a pan of boiling water until tender. For the rosti, grate the white potatoes, squeezing out any juice as you go. Place the grated potato in a lint-free tea towel, pull the corners together and really squeeze out as much liquid as you can. Season the potato with salt.

Heat the olive oil in a non-stick pan (the more you use, the crispier the rosti will be) and if you are using metal cooking rings, oil the insides of those. Start frying the grated potato in 4 portions, either shaped into rounds with a spoon or cooked inside the metal rings. Lightly press down with a spoon or spatula to make sure the rosti cook evenly. They should need about 5 minutes on each side. Fry until they are crispy and golden.

Meanwhile, crumble the silken tofu into a bowl until it looks like scrambled egg. Stir in the nutritional yeast flakes, half of the black salt and the turmeric (this gives the tofu a sulphurous 'eggy' flavour and yellow colour respectively). Give it a good stir before baking the mixture on the tray in the oven or frying it gently in a pan on the hob.

While the other elements are cooking, purée the cooked sweet potato in a blender with a little of the cooking water, a really good glug of olive oil and the remaining black salt. This is your 'egg yolk' style sauce.

In a separate pan, wilt the spinach and season with salt to taste. Remove the roasted tomatoes and mushrooms from the oven, take the scrambled tofu off the heat and keep everything warm.

When your rosti are golden on both sides, remove from the pan and dry them on some kitchen paper. Put one on each plate and top with wilted spinach, then scrambled tofu, sweet potato sauce, mushrooms and tomatoes.

EXOTIC MUSHROOMS AND SPINACH WITH CASHEW CRUMBS

Preparation time: 5 minutes
Cooking time: 20 minutes
Serves 2
Gluten-free when using gluten-free bread

A simple and delicious breakfast. I use cooking spinach rather than baby spinach because it holds together better, does not lose too much water and has a really good flavour. If you are using king oyster mushrooms, put them in the pan first for 2 minutes as they take a little longer to cook.

25g cashews

2 good handfuls of exotic mushrooms (such chanterelles, oyster, king oyster and a few enoki)

1 clove of garlic

Olive oil

100g cooking spinach, washed and dried then sliced

Truffle oil (optional)

Salt and pepper

Sourdough, to serve

Preheat your oven to 150°c. Place the cashews on a baking tray and toast them in the hot oven for 10 minutes. Take them out and give them a stir, then return the tray to the oven and check again after 5 minutes. You want them to be golden but neither dark nor pale. When done, remove the toasted cashews from the oven and leave to cool before breaking up with a rolling pin. The neatest way to do this is by wrapping them in a tea towel or sealed plastic bag before bashing into crumbs.

Meanwhile, make sure the mushrooms are clean and brush off any dirt if necessary. Cut them into evenly sized pieces, leaving the smaller ones whole. Crush the clove of garlic with the back of a knife and peel off the skin, then cut the clove in half.

Heat a little olive oil in a non-stick pan, add the garlic and cook for about 90 seconds to flavour the oil. Now turn up the heat and add the mushrooms. Cook for about 5 minutes, stirring continuously. Next, make sure all the water has been removed from the spinach and add it to the pan of mushrooms. Cook for another 3 minutes until the spinach has wilted.

Finally, stir in some truffle oil (approximately 1 teaspoon, or to taste) and season the mushroom mixture with salt and pepper.

Serve the mushrooms on some really good, toasted sourdough and sprinkle over your toasted cashew crumbs.

PECAN, CHERRY AND COCONUT GRANOLA

Preparation time: 5 minutes

Cooking time: 40-50 minutes

Makes enough to fill a 2 litre container

Gluten-free when using gluten-free oats

A delicious, easy recipe that fills the whole house with a wonderful aroma. Cook low and slow until it develops a deep golden hue (any darker and it will taste bitter). If you do not mind upping the sugar content a little bit more it will form into clusters.

125ml maple syrup

25g white sugar

25ml coconut oil

1 teaspoon vanilla extract

500g jumbo rolled oats

175g mixed seeds

75g desiccated coconut

25g flaked almonds

150g pecans

100g dried cherries

Preheat the oven to 160°c and line 2 large trays with baking paper. Place the maple syrup, sugar, coconut oil and vanilla extract into a large bowl and mix well. Now toss in the oats, seeds, coconut and almonds. Stir until everything is coated evenly, then distribute the granola mix between the prepared trays. Spread out to form even layers and place in the preheated oven.

Bake the granola for about 15 minutes, then stir in the pecans and swap the trays over. Continue to bake the granola, stirring every 10 minutes and swapping the trays as needed, until it has turned golden brown and dried out to form small clumps. This should take about 40 minutes, but ovens do vary quite dramatically so you may need to keep baking until the granola reaches your desired consistency.

Leave the baked granola to cool, then stir in the dried cherries. This mixture can now be kept in an airtight container for up to 1 month. Serve with vegan yoghurt and plenty of fresh berries.

VANILLA POACHED RHUBARB PORRIDGE

Preparation time: 15 minutes
Cooking time: 15-20 minutes
Serves 4
Gluten-free when using gluten-free oats

This recipe came about when we ran a competition at the café for the team to come up with a new porridge recipe, won by Jye the Aussie barista who developed this. It's very easy to make when good rhubarb is in season and a firm favourite in the Pearce household.

Handful of sunflower seeds (optional)

200g rhubarb, chopped evenly

80g white sugar or agave syrup

1 teaspoon vanilla paste

A little orange zest, to taste

100ml water

200g porridge oats

800ml oat milk

1 tablespoon maple syrup

Preheat your oven to approximately 160°c if you are using the sunflower seeds as a garnish. Place them on a baking tray and toast in the preheated oven for about 15 to 20 minutes, until they turn a light golden colour.

Place the rhubarb in a pan with the sugar, vanilla, orange zest and water. Poach gently with a lid on until the rhubarb is soft. It will take about 10 minutes until the rhubarb is starting to soften but still has a little shape.

Meanwhile, combine the oats, milk and syrup in another saucepan. Bring to a gentle boil and cook for 5 minutes until the oats are tender, stirring regularly.

Divide the porridge between bowls and top with your poached rhubarb, then garnish with some seasonal berries, edible flowers and a scattering of toasted sunflower seeds if you like.

VEGAN FLUFFY PANCAKES WITH BERRY COMPOTE

Preparation time: 15 minutes
Cooking time: 20 minutes
Serves 4 (makes 8 pancakes)

This delicious recipe is a real weekend treat. Who said vegan food can't be indulgent? I make this for unsuspecting omnivore guests all the time and nobody ever guesses it's all plant-based!

For the pancakes

425g soya milk

10ml apple cider vinegar

190g rice flour

180g self-raising flour

10g bicarbonate of soda

2 tablespoons white sugar

Pinch of salt

50g coconut oil

2 teaspoons vanilla paste

For the compote

2 punnets of fresh or frozen mixed berries (approximately 400g)

1 tablespoon white sugar

1/4 teaspoon vanilla paste, or a few drops of real vanilla extract

For the pancakes

Mix the soya milk and apple cider vinegar together, then leave to stand for 10 minutes. In a separate bowl, combine all the dry ingredients.

Add the coconut oil and vanilla paste to the soya milk mixture, then pour this into the bowl of dry ingredients and whisk vigorously to ensure there are no lumps. Leave to rest for 5 minutes.

For the compote

While the pancake batter is resting, place all the ingredients into a small saucepan and cook on a low heat for 10 minutes until the berries start to burst and release their juices. If you want a slightly thicker compote, add a little more sugar. It's perfect with these pancakes of course but can also be served warm with porridge or chilled with a nice cheesecake for dessert.

To cook the pancakes

Gently heat a small amount of neutral oil in a non-stick pan. Pour in enough batter to make your preferred size of pancake, and fry until the underside is a light golden colour before flipping. Repeat until all the batter is used up, and serve the pancakes warm with the compote and/or maple syrup.

Small Plates

AJO BLANCO
(SPANISH CHILLED ALMOND SOUP)

Preparation time: 10 minutes, plus overnight
Serves 4

I just love this cold soup. It's easy to make, healthy and tasty on a hot summer's day. It's important to get a good quality sherry vinegar and olive oil, as these are central flavours in the dish.

250g blanched almonds, soaked in water overnight

100g crusty white bread, left out to dry overnight

750ml iced water

1 clove of garlic

100g white grapes

75ml good quality olive oil

6 tablespoons sherry vinegar

Salt, to taste

Toasted flaked almonds, to serve

Drain the soaked almonds and cut the dry bread into cubes. Place the almonds, iced water and peeled garlic in a food processor. Blend well, then add the cubed bread and white grapes. Blend again until smooth, season with salt to taste, then blend in the olive oil. Add the sherry vinegar to taste, until the balance is right for you. Check the seasoning and refrigerate until cold before serving. Garnish the ajo blanco with some lightly toasted flaked almonds and an extra drizzle of olive oil.

ASPARAGUS AND GREEN PEA FARINATA

Preparation time: 10 minutes
Cooking time: 10 minutes
Serves 2
Gluten-free

Farinata, sometimes called socca, is an unleavened chickpea flour pancake that originated in Genoa, Italy. Traditionally it's made with just chickpea flour, water, olive oil and salt but we have added a few spring veggies and a little rosemary to give it some freshness.

125g chickpea flour

200ml water

50ml olive oil

$1/2$ teaspoon fine sea salt

A few sprigs of rosemary, finely chopped

1 bunch of asparagus, finely sliced

Handful of frozen peas

Cherry tomatoes (optional)

Olives (optional)

Whisk the chickpea flour, water, olive oil and salt together until there are no lumps, then stir in the rosemary. This is your batter.

Heat a non-stick frying with a small amount of olive oil in it. Fry the sliced asparagus and peas for a couple of minutes before pouring in the batter. Fry until sealed and then flip over and cook on the other side for a minute.

You could serve the farinata with some gently pan-fried cherry tomatoes and olives if you like.

BANG BANG CAULIFLOWER WITH PICKLED VEGETABLES

Preparation time: 30 minutes, plus 4 hours pickling
Cooking time: 10 minutes
Serves 4 as a starter
Gluten-free

The original version of this recipe was brought to us by the fantastic chef Matt from Demuths Cookery School here in Bath. This is one of our most popular dishes with customers and the team. You can scale up the sauce recipe as it will keep well in the freezer.

For the pickled vegetables

250g cucumber

250g daikon radish

250g carrots

2 tablespoons fine sea salt

50g white sugar

200ml white rice vinegar

For the tempura cauliflower

1 whole large cauliflower

25g rice flour

15g cornflour

1 tablespoon chickpea flour

50ml water

For the mirin and gochujang sauce

A little sunflower oil

5 cloves of garlic

25g gochujang paste

90ml tamari

40ml mirin

60g brown sugar

330ml water

25g cornflour

For the garnish

Spring onions, chopped

Sesame seeds, toasted

Fresh chilli, sliced

For the pickled vegetables

Halve the cucumber lengthways and remove the soft seeded centre with a teaspoon. Peel the radish and carrots, then cut all the vegetables into thin sticks about 4cm long. Place them in a colander or sieve, sprinkle over the salt and leave to drain for 1 hour.

Gently squeeze any remaining juice out of the salted vegetables and place them in an airtight container. Whisk the sugar and rice vinegar together in a bowl until the sugar has completely dissolved. Pour this liquid over the vegetables and leave in the fridge overnight. Alternatively, you could heat the vinegar and sugar mixture gently before pouring it over the vegetables and then leave for a few hours to speed up the process. The pickled vegetables will keep in the fridge for 3 months.

For the tempura cauliflower

Separate the cauliflower florets and cut them into neat halves, or quarters if large. Combine all the flours and mix well, then add the water and whisk thoroughly, making sure there are no lumps. Heat a deep fryer or pan of oil to 170°c. Dip the cauliflower pieces into the batter until fully coated, then deep fry in the hot oil for 3 minutes until they are sealed and cooked a little. Remove from the oil and drain on kitchen paper.

For the mirin and gochujang sauce

Heat the oil in a pan while you mince the garlic in a food processor. Fry the garlic in the hot oil until lightly golden, then stir in the gochujang paste and fry for a couple more minutes. Add the tamari, mirin, sugar and 300ml of the water and then bring the mixture to the boil. Make a paste with the cornflour and remaining water in a small bowl, then whisk this paste into the boiling sauce and take the pan off the heat.

If you intend to eat straight away, add the battered cauliflower to the sauce and stir to coat all the pieces. Cook the cauliflower in the sauce for a couple of minutes until the florets are well coated and the sauce has been absorbed by the batter.

Serve the bang bang cauliflower with pickled vegetables of your choice and garnish the dish with some chopped spring onions, toasted sesame seeds and a little fresh chilli if you feel like it.

CELERIAC FRITTERS WITH DILL AND TARRAGON REMOULADE

Preparation time: 15 minutes
Cooking time: 15 minutes
Serves 6-8
Gluten-free

Use this batter recipe as a base for nearly any quick-cooking vegetable to make more variations on these quick and easy fritters. Remoulade is a French mayonnaise-based sauce, similar to tartare sauce, that is served cold and provides a great contrast to the hot fritters.

For the fritters

200g chickpea flour

50g cornflour

$1/2$ teaspoon paprika

$1/2$ teaspoon smoked paprika

$1/2$ teaspoon ground fennel

$1/2$ teaspoon nutmeg

200ml water

1 teaspoon salt

250g celeriac, finely diced

1 small red onion, finely diced

1 large stick of celery, finely diced

For the remoulade

5cm cucumber, halved and deseeded

1 small shallot, peeled and chopped

$1^{1}/2$ tablespoons capers

$1^{1}/2$ tablespoons chopped fresh dill

1 tablespoon chopped fresh tarragon

$1^{1}/2$ tablespoons Dijon mustard

100g vegan mayonnaise (see page 174)

Sift the flours and spices for the fritters into a large bowl, then add the water and whisk well until there are no lumps. Stir in the salt and then let the batter sit for 15 minutes.

Meanwhile, make the remoulade by pulsing all the ingredients except the mayonnaise in a food processor until coarsely blended. You want the remoulade to have a little texture. Stir in the mayonnaise and chill until serving.

Once the batter has rested, heat a deep pan of oil or deep fat fryer to 180°c. Fold the diced vegetables into the batter when you are ready to start frying, mixing well to coat them thoroughly.

Using 2 tablespoons, one to scoop up the fritter mix and the other to slide it into the hot oil, carefully start to fry the fritters. Add a few spoonfuls to the fryer at a time, making sure it doesn't get too crowded. They should take 3 or 4 minutes to cook right through, depending on their size. Remove the fritters from the oil with a slotted spoon and place on kitchen paper to drain.

If you are not planning to serve the fritters straight away, fry them for about 90 seconds until they are sealed, then remove and drain. They will keep well in the fridge or freezer and can then be finished at a later date by deep frying in hot oil from chilled or frozen.

Serve the hot fritters with your dill and tarragon remoulade.

GAZPACHO

Preparation time: 15 minutes, plus at least
1 hour chilling
Serves 4

I could drink this soup every day for the rest of my life; I love it! Garnish with finely diced peppers and red onion, a drizzle of really good olive oil and croutons if you like.

6 medium vine tomatoes (the riper the better)

1 clove of garlic

1 red pepper

1 cucumber

1 shallot

100ml iced water

100g stale bread, crusts removed (optional)

Salt and pepper

2 tablespoons good quality sherry vinegar, or to taste

125ml extra virgin olive oil

Bring a pan of water to the boil while you score a cross at the bottom of each tomato with a sharp knife. Submerge the tomatoes in the boiling water for about a minute. You want to see the skin slightly peeling away from the incision you have made. Remove them from the water and place in a colander to cool slightly before peeling off the skins using your fingers.

Quarter the peeled tomatoes, scrape out all the seeds and put the remaining flesh into a powerful blender. Crush the garlic with the flat side of your knife blade and remove the skin, then chop into a few pieces. Halve, deseed and slice the pepper. Peel and roughly chop the cucumber. Slice the shallot and rinse under cold water. Place all the prepared ingredients into the blender along with the iced water and blend on a high speed until the mixture is really smooth.

If you are adding bread to your gazpacho, now is the time. Leave the cubed bread to soak in the blended mixture for 10 minutes before blending again.

Season the soup with salt and pepper, then add the sherry vinegar, using slightly more or less according to your taste. Blend the gazpacho on a slow speed while gradually adding the olive oil.

Taste the gazpacho and adjust the salt and vinegar as needed. If the texture is too thick for your liking, add some more cold water. Refrigerate the soup for at least an hour and serve cold. Garnish with finely diced peppers, red onion, croutons and freshly ground black pepper.

GLUTEN-FREE BEER BATTERED ONION RINGS

Preparation time: 15 minutes, plus 3 hours marinating
Cooking time: 15 minutes
Serves 2-4
Gluten-free

We strived for many a day and night to come up with a recipe for gluten-free onion rings. The preparation time is well worth it! They also freeze well once sealed if you want to make a larger batch and can be fried straight from frozen.

2 large Spanish onions

250ml white wine vinegar

150g white rice four, plus extra for dusting

50g chickpea flour, plus extra for dusting

50g farina (potato flour)

50g cornflour

4 teaspoons onion powder

2 teaspoons fine salt

1 teaspoon white pepper

300ml gluten-free beer

Oil, for frying (such as sunflower or rapeseed)

Peel the onions whole, then slice them evenly into 1cm rounds and remove the centres. Place the onion slices in a 2 litre container, cover with water and pour in the white wine vinegar. Leave to soak for at least 3 hours (overnight is ideal). If preferred, you can omit the white wine vinegar completely and just soak them in water. Personally, I like the taste because it's reminiscent of pickled onions which cuts through the oil well.

Transfer the marinated onion slices to a colander and separate the slices into rings, allowing them to drain thoroughly. Meanwhile, sift all the flours into a large bowl. Stir in the onion powder, salt and white pepper and then pour in two thirds of the beer. Whisk until the batter is smooth with no lumps, then slowly add the remaining beer while whisking until it reaches a consistency like double cream (vegan obviously!) or a thick pancake batter, still a little runny but not so much that it doesn't stick to the onions.

If you do not have a dedicated deep fat fryer, heat half a pan of oil to 180°c. The saucepan should be deep and the oil should not come much further than halfway up the sides for safety reasons. Ideally, you should also use a wire mesh basket or spoon to remove things from the fryer.

In another bowl, combine the extra rice flour and chickpea flour. Put the onion rings on a baking tray and dust each one with a little of the flour. Dip just enough onion rings to fit in your pan or fryer (probably 6 to 8) into the batter using metal tongs. Give them a gentle shake to remove the excess, then carefully lower them into the hot oil and cook in batches for 3 minutes before transferring the fried onion rings to a plate or tray lined with kitchen paper.

Repeat this process with all your onion rings and batter, adding a little more beer towards the end if the batter has thickened up with the extra flour. A very dense batter will not stick to the onions.

If you want to freeze the onion rings, deep fry them just long enough to seal the batter (90 seconds) and then drain before storing and freezing. They can then be fried from frozen.

Season the hot battered onion rings with some Maldon sea salt. Enjoy with some vegan mayonnaise on the side for dipping (see page 174).

MUSHROOM AND ALMOND SOUP

Preparation time: 15 minutes, plus soaking
overnight (optional)
Cooking time: 45 minutes
Serves 4
Gluten-free

This delicious autumn and winter soup is very popular in the café. You can skip soaking the almonds overnight if you are short on time; the soup will just have a slightly grainy texture.

20g dried porcini mushrooms (optional)

150g ground almonds

200ml sherry

Olive oil

2 medium onions, finely diced

2 sticks of celery, finely diced

4 cloves of garlic, minced

10g fresh thyme leaves

250g chestnut mushrooms, sliced

2 litres vegetable stock

Salt and pepper

Put the dried mushrooms (if using) and ground almonds in a bowl with a little water, just enough to cover them by 1cm. Add the sherry and leave to soak overnight. Do not discard the liquid.

Heat a little olive oil in a pan and cook the finely diced onion and celery on a medium heat until they are starting to turn golden. Now add the minced garlic and fresh thyme leaves and cook for another 2 minutes before adding the sliced mushrooms.

Cook the mixture for about 5 minutes, then pour in the soaked almonds and mushrooms along with all the soaking liquid. Now add the stock and cook on a medium heat for 30 minutes.

Remove any thyme stalks from the soup before transferring it to a blender. Blend until really smooth, then taste and season with salt and a good twist of black pepper. Serve hot.

PAELLA ARANCINI WITH ALMOND AIOLI

Preparation time: 15 minutes, plus 1 hour chilling
Cooking time: 30 minutes
Serves 4-6

This is another recipe that we created by accident when experimenting with leftover paella. Traditionally, arancini have mozzarella inside them, so if you want to put a cube of some melty vegan cheese inside this version, go ahead.

For the arancini

1 onion

1 red pepper

1 green pepper

Olive oil

1 teaspoon chopped fresh rosemary

6 cloves of garlic, finely chopped

1 tablespoon tomato purée

1 teaspoon sweet paprika

250g risotto rice

750ml hot vegetable stock

Pinch of saffron

100g breadcrumbs

For the almond aioli

100g blanched almonds

10 white seedless grapes

1 clove of garlic, peeled

3 tablespoons olive oil

2 tablespoons sherry vinegar

1 tablespoon lemon juice

175g vegan mayonnaise (see page 174)

For the arancini

Dice the onion and peppers as finely as you can. The finer the dice of these vegetables, the easier the arancini will be to roll. Heat a little olive oil in a large heavy-bottomed pan and gently sauté the onion, pepper, rosemary and garlic until soft.

Add the tomato purée and paprika, fry for a couple of minutes, then stir in the rice. Fry for another minute or so, stirring regularly. Test the temperature with the back of your fingers. When the rice is becoming too hot to touch, add one third of the hot stock and the saffron. Keep stirring with a wooden spoon to avoid the rice sticking to the bottom of the pan.

Continue adding the stock a ladleful at a time and stir continuously. Wait until the stock has been absorbed into the rice before adding the next batch. Repeat this process until all the liquid has been absorbed and the rice has the slightest bite to it. It will keep cooking slightly after you have removed it from the pan. You may not need to use all the stock so do not add it all unnecessarily, otherwise you may end up with soggy, overcooked rice. When the paella is ready, spread it out on a large tray and leave to cool and set in the fridge for at least 1 hour.

For the almond aioli

While the rice is cooling, make the almond aioli. Simply blend all the ingredients except the mayonnaise together until puréed. Mix in the mayo and stir well to combine. Chill before serving.

To assemble and serve

Roll the chilled paella into balls approximately 6cm in diameter. Spread the breadcrumbs out on a plate. You can use gluten-free panko breadcrumbs here, which taste just as good. Roll the balls of rice in the breadcrumbs until they are completely coated.

Meanwhile, heat up a deep fat fryer or a deep saucepan half filled with vegetable oil to 180°c. If you do not have a thermometer, drop in a small piece of bread and check whether it rises to the surface quickly and bubbles rapidly. If it does, the oil is ready. Fry each arancini a few at a time until the breadcrumb coating is golden. Remove with a slotted spoon and place on kitchen paper to drain.

Serve the hot arancini with the almond aioli alongside for dipping.

POTATO BONDA

Preparation time: 15 minutes
Cooking time: 30 minutes
Serves 4-6
Gluten-free

This popular South Indian street food snack is also known as aloo bonda, and can include various different ingredients according to the regional cuisines in which it's found. They're especially good dipped into our coconut chutney (see page 155) or tomato chutney (see page 166).

For the batter

125g chickpea flour

50g cornflour or white rice flour

1/2 teaspoon ground turmeric

1/2 teaspoon chilli powder

Pinch of salt, to taste

140ml water

For the filling

5 medium-sized Maris Piper potatoes

2 teaspoons brown mustard seeds

1 small onion, finely diced

2 green chillies, deseeded and finely chopped

2 tablespoons grated fresh ginger

1 tablespoon garlic purée

15 fresh curry leaves, finely sliced

2 teaspoons ajwain seeds

2 tablespoons desiccated coconut

1 tablespoons lemon juice

Salt and pepper

Oil, for frying

Peel and chop the potatoes and then boil gently in salted water until just done. Do not overcook them here. If needed, you can dry out the potatoes on a tray in a hot oven for a couple of minutes. Mash the potatoes until smooth with no lumps, then set aside to cool.

Prepare the batter by combining all the ingredients in a large bowl. Whisk thoroughly until there are no lumps. It should taste slightly salty.

Heat a few tablespoons of oil in a frying pan, then add the mustard seeds and let them pop. Add the finely diced onion and fry until golden, then stir in the green chilli, ginger, garlic, curry leaves and ajwain seeds. Cook for another minute before stirring this mixture into the mashed potato along with the coconut and lemon juice. Mix well, then taste and season with salt and pepper if needed.

Heat your oil in a deep fat fryer until it gets to about 175°c. Roll the potato mixture into golf ball sized spheres, dip them into the batter using a spoon, roll around in your hand and then deep fry in batches until sealed and dark golden. Drain on kitchen paper to remove the excess oil, then serve warm with chutney of your choice.

PUMPKIN AND CELERIAC SAMOSAS

Preparation time: 25 minutes
Cooking time: 1 hour
Serves 6

This Indian street food snack is an absolute classic and so delicious served with our tamarind sauce (see page 168). The main thing to remember is not to overwork the dough otherwise it will be hard rather than flaky; it only needs to be brought together with a brief kneading.

For the pastry

175g plain flour

80g semolina

1 teaspoon ajwain seeds (optional)

1/2 teaspoon fine salt

100g vegetable fat, softened

50ml iced water

For the filling

150g celeriac, finely diced

150g pumpkin, finely diced

1 floury potato, finely diced

1/2 tablespoon brown mustard seeds

1 green chilli, deseeded and finely chopped

5g fresh ginger, peeled and minced

1/2 teaspoon asafoetida (hing)

1/2 teaspoon chilli powder (optional)

4 tablespoons frozen peas (optional)

To make the samosas

Oil, for frying

1/2 tablespoon chaat masala

For the pastry

Blend the flour, semolina, ajwain seeds and salt in a mixing bowl. Rub in the softened fat with your fingertips until it is fully incorporated and the mixture resembles breadcrumbs. Add the iced water and work in until the dough can be gathered into a ball. Knead for a minute or so on a clean surface until the dough is smooth and pliable. Reshape into a ball, rub with a little oil, wrap in cling film and leave to rest in the fridge for 45 minutes.

For the filling

Whilst the dough is resting, roast the pumpkin and celeriac in the oven for about 30 to 40 minutes until soft but not browned. Keep them at separate ends of the tin because the celeriac may take a little longer. Meanwhile, boil or steam the potato until tender, then drain and mash.

Heat some oil in a pan and fry the mustard seeds until they begin to pop. Add the green chilli, ginger and asafoetida to fry for 1 minute before stirring in the roasted pumpkin and celeriac. Mash the mixture a little with a fork. Stir in the remaining ingredients, including the mashed potato, and season with salt to taste. Allow the filling to cool a little before assembling the samosas.

To make the samosas

Unwrap the rested dough and give it a quick knead to loosen it up a little. Divide the dough into 6 equal pieces. Roll each one out with a rolling pin to about 15cm (6 inches) in diameter, then cut in half to form semicircles. Dampen the straight edges with a little water, then bring the two ends together so they overlap slightly and form a cone shape, pinching the seams together to seal it. Spoon the filling into the cones, leaving a 1cm gap at the top so you can pinch the dough together and seal it closed. Cover the finished samosas with a damp cloth while you make the others.

Heat your oil to a low temperature in a large pan or deep fat fryer. Cook the samosas for about 8 minutes until they are a light golden brown, then turn up the temperature to finish them. If you cook them straight away on a high heat they will blister, and the dough will not be cooked through.

Drain the samosas on kitchen paper, then sprinkle over the chaat masala and serve hot with tamarind sauce on the side for dipping.

QUINOA TABBOULEH

Preparation time: 10 minutes
Cooking time: 15 minutes
Serves 4
Gluten-free

Tabbouleh is a traditional Lebanese parsley salad normally made with bulgur wheat. We have swapped the bulgur for quinoa so it can be gluten-free. It's a staple component of any mezze and has gained worldwide popularity.

100g quinoa

45ml lemon juice

50g flat leaf parsley, sliced

15g fresh mint leaves, finely sliced

2 ripe vine tomatoes, deseeded and finely chopped

3 spring onions, sliced

3 tablespoons olive oil

Salt, to taste

Place the quinoa in a sieve and give it a rinse under cold running water. Transfer it to a small pan with a lid and pour in 125ml of water. Bring to the boil and simmer gently for 10 minutes until the water has evaporated. Stir the quinoa and put the lid back on. Leave to stand for 5 minutes before transferring to a tray to cool off.

When the quinoa is cool, mix in all the remaining ingredients until they are well incorporated and serve the tabbouleh at room temperature.

STEAMED ASPARAGUS
WITH RAW ROMESCO SALSA

Preparation time: 15 minutes,
plus 30 minutes soaking
Serves 4
Gluten-free

Romesco is usually served with fish and meat but I like it with veggies, raw or cooked, especially steamed asparagus. This is a raw version; traditionally you would use roasted peppers and roasted almonds, which is just as delicious but takes a little longer.

20g whole sun-dried tomatoes

35g blanched almonds

1 red pepper, deseeded and chopped

1 clove of garlic, peeled

3 tablespoons olive oil

1 tablespoon fresh lemon juice

1/2 tablespoon agave syrup

Salt, to taste

3 bunches of asparagus

First, soak the sun-dried tomatoes in hot water for 20 minutes and then drain well. Blend the blanched almonds in a food processor until they are between coarse and fine in texture, then transfer to a large bowl. Place the drained tomatoes into the food processor with all the remaining ingredients except the asparagus and then blend until the salsa is fairly smooth. Add this to the bowl of almonds and stir, taste and season with salt.

Snap off the bottom end of each asparagus spear with your fingers (there should be a natural breaking point approximately 4cm up) and then steam the spears gently for about 4 minutes. Serve with the raw salsa.

SPANISH ARTICHOKES
IN ALMOND SAUCE

Preparation time: 10 minutes
Cooking time: 20 minutes
Serves 4-6

In this recipe I have used the pre-cooked artichokes that you can buy from any good delicatessen, just to save some time and effort. The sauce has a delightful creamy white wine flavour. Best served with some crusty fresh bread.

750g jarred cooked artichokes

6 tablespoons olive oil

2 shallots, finely diced

2 cloves of garlic, finely chopped

1 lemon, juiced

200ml white wine

500ml good quality stock

Salt and pepper

1 slice of good white bread

70g blanched almonds

Good quality paprika or smoked paprika

Slice the artichokes in half lengthways to keep their beautiful shape, rinse off any excess oil if they are marinated and set aside.

Heat half of the olive oil in a heavy-bottomed saucepan and fry the diced shallot on a medium heat until a slight colour develops. Stir in the chopped garlic and cook for another 2 minutes. Pour in the lemon juice and white wine, bring to the boil and then cook off the alcohol for a few minutes. Add the stock, stir well and season with salt and pepper. Cook for about 10 minutes to reduce a little.

Meanwhile, heat the remaining olive oil in another saucepan and fry the bread on both sides until golden. Transfer the bread into a heavy pestle and mortar along with the blanched almonds and mash them together until a paste forms.

Add this paste to the first pan along with the prepared artichokes and simmer gently for 5 minutes, or until the sauce has thickened. Remove from the heat and allow to cool slightly before dividing between bowls. Sprinkle with some good quality regular or smoked paprika (it's up to you) and then serve with your favourite bread.

If you are not serving the dish straight away, the sauce will thicken up as it cools so just loosen it with a little water or stock in the pan when reheating. Taste and recheck the seasoning too.

SQUASH AND GINGER PAKORAS WITH WATERCRESS RAITA

Preparation time: 15 minutes
Cooking time: 10 minutes
Serves 4-6
Gluten-free

Fiery ginger and sweet squash work so well together in these deep-fried Indian snacks. You could use other types of squash or pumpkin instead of the butternut if preferred, and any vegan yoghurt will work in place of the soya for the raita.

For the raita

250g soya yoghurt

50g watercress leaves

1 small green chilli (optional)

1 small clove of garlic

A few fresh mint leaves

1/2 teaspoon ground cumin

1/2 teaspoon white sugar

1/2 teaspoon salt

For the pakoras

Oil, for frying

160g chickpea flour

40g cornflour

1 teaspoon ground cumin

1 teaspoon garam masala

1/2 teaspoon chilli powder

1/2 teaspoon ground turmeric

1 teaspoon salt

150g water

500g butternut squash

50g fresh ginger

1 small red onion

A few fresh coriander leaves

For the raita

Place all the ingredients into a food processor and blend until fairly smooth, with a few green specks still visible. It can also be made by hand and left chunky; finely slice the leaves and chilli if using, crush the garlic to a purée with the back of a knife and some salt, then stir everything together.

For the pakoras

Heat a deep fat fryer or a large saucepan of oil to around 180°c. First, make the batter. Combine the flours, spices and salt before mixing in the water until smooth. Let it rest while you prepare the other ingredients.

Peel the squash and cut each end off, then cut lengthways and remove all the seeds. I find a dessert spoon works best for this. Cut each half into 3 or 4 pieces so they can then be easily grated by hand or with a grating attachment in a food processor. Grate the ginger on a fine side of a grater or by using a microplane. Peel and finely slice the red onion.

Now stir the grated ginger and squash, sliced red onion and coriander leaves into the batter. Use 2 spoons to form the pakoras and drop them carefully into the hot oil one by one. Fry until they are dark golden. You must fry the pakoras immediately after the vegetables have been added, otherwise they will leak water and the batter will become too thin. Drain the pakoras on kitchen paper and then serve warm with the watercress raita.

TANDOORI KING OYSTER MUSHROOMS, KACHUMBER SALAD AND MINT RAITA

Preparation time: 15 minutes, plus 1 hour
marinating
Cooking time: 25 minutes
Serves 4-6
Gluten-free

This tandoori dish is great fresh from the oven or on the barbecue. The accompanying Indian salad is deliberately simple. It is used as a cooling accompaniment to hot dishes alongside the creamy raita, which is another very quick recipe taught to me by my Indian head chef Shamim in New Zealand.

500g king oyster mushrooms

3 cloves of garlic

1 thumb-sized piece of fresh ginger

1 green chilli

2 tablespoons mustard oil (optional)

1 tablespoon tomato purée

2 teaspoons each amchoor (dried mango powder) and ground cumin

1 teaspoon each ground coriander, garam masala, mild smoked paprika, paprika and salt

50ml fresh lime juice

350g vegan yoghurt

Fresh coriander leaves, to garnish

For the kachumber salad

1 small cucumber

1 red onion

2 tomatoes

1/2 lemon, juiced

1 teaspoon chaat masala

Salt and pepper

For the raita

1 small shallot

5cm cucumber

A few fresh mint and coriander leaves

250g vegan yoghurt

1/2 teaspoon each ground cumin and white sugar

Pinch of salt

Trim the very bottom off the king oyster mushrooms as this bit can be quite tough. Slice them lengthways, then score the insides in a cross pattern with a sharp knife to help the marinade soak in. Purée the garlic by crushing the cloves with the back of a knife and some salt, finely grate the ginger, finely chop the chilli (deseeding if you prefer less heat) and put them into a bowl. Stir in all the remaining ingredients except the fresh coriander and mix together thoroughly.

Pour the yoghurt marinade over the prepared mushrooms and leave them to marinate for at least an hour, ideally overnight. Bake the marinated mushrooms in a preheated oven at 180°c for about 25 minutes or until they start to brown at the edges. Garnish with the coriander leaves when done.

For the kachumber salad

Slice the cucumber lengthways and scrape out the seeds with a teaspoon. Finely dice the red onion, place in a sieve and rinse under the tap for a minute. Core and deseed the tomatoes, then finely dice them along with the cucumber and place in a small bowl. Mix in the rinsed red onion, stir in the lemon juice and sprinkle over the chaat masala. Add a little salt and pepper to taste.

For the raita

Finely dice the shallot, grate the cucumber and roughly chop the mint and coriander. Mix all the ingredients together in a bowl and serve alongside the tandoori mushrooms and kachumber salad.

Large Plates

AUTHENTIC THAI RED CURRY

Preparation time: 30-40 minutes
Cooking time: 20-30 minutes
Serves 4
Gluten-free

This is as authentic as it gets; I learned how to make it in Thailand on one of many trips out there. Try to find a traditional Thai coconut milk and always use fresh kaffir lime leaves (the dried ones are dreadful, no flavour at all). They keep well in the freezer if you need to buy larger quantities.

For the paste

10 large dried red chillies

10 fresh bird's eye chillies

15g shallot

15g garlic

10g galangal

10g fresh lemongrass (lower section only)

5g kaffir lime peel (or regular lime if you cannot get it)

5g coriander root (optional)

1 teaspoon ground coriander

1 teaspoon ground cardamom

1/2 teaspoon black pepper

1/2 teaspoon salt

For the curry

3 tablespoons oil

3 tablespoons red Thai curry paste (see above)

750ml good quality coconut milk

1 carrot, sliced

100g baby corn

100g tenderstem broccoli

100g bamboo shoots

150g tofu, deep fried

30ml soy sauce (or vegan fish sauce if you have it)

3 fresh kaffir lime leaves, finely sliced

1 tablespoon coconut sugar

Thai basil leaves

For the paste

First, remove the seeds from the dried red chillies and soak them in a bowl of water for 30 minutes. Reduce the number of bird's eye chillies if you prefer less spicy curries. Meanwhile, peel the shallot, garlic and galangal and weigh out all the fresh ingredients.

Drain the soaked chillies and place them in a heavy pestle and mortar or a high-powered blender with all the other ingredients. Pound or blend to a fairly smooth paste.

For the curry

Heat the oil in a wok and fry the red curry paste for 3 to 4 minutes. If it starts to stick, add a little of the coconut milk.

Once the paste has cooked through, add the remainder of the coconut milk and heat it to boiling point before adding all the vegetables.

Cook until the vegetables are al dente, then stir in the deep fried tofu, soy sauce, lime leaves and sugar. Garnish with some fresh Thai basil leaves and serve the curry with jasmine rice.

BANANA BLOSSOM 'FISH' WITH MINTED PEA PURÉE

Preparation time: 15 minutes, plus at least 1 hour marinating
Cooking time: 10 minutes
Serves 4-6

This delicious alternative to fried fish is perfect served with our twice-cooked chips and plum ketchup. If you can't find nori sprinkles, just finely chop some nori sheets instead.

For the 'fish'

1 tin of banana blossom (500g)

2 tablespoons nori sprinkle

100g plain flour

100g cornflour

1/2 teaspoon baking powder

1/2 teaspoon ground turmeric

1/2 teaspoon nori sprinkles

250ml beer or sparkling water

For the minted pea purée

1 shallot, finely diced

1 tablespoon olive oil

250g frozen peas

125ml soya milk (or any other alternative milk)

Pinch of salt

A few fresh mint leaves

To serve

Twice-cooked chips (see page 78)

Plum ketchup (see page 164)

For the 'fish'

First, drain the banana blossom and rinse it gently with cold water, then place in an airtight container, sprinkle on the 2 tablespoons of nori and leave in the fridge for at least 1 hour (ideally overnight). The nori will add the flavour of the sea to your 'fish'.

To make the batter, whisk the remaining dry ingredients (flours, baking powder, turmeric, nori) together in a bowl, then pour in the liquid and whisk well until combined. It should be a thick batter that's ready to use right away.

When you are ready to fry the fish, heat some rapeseed oil in a deep fat fryer or deep pan to 180°c. If you do not have a thermometer, place a small piece of bread into the oil. When it bubbles rapidly on the surface, your oil is hot enough.

Pat each piece of marinated banana blossom with some kitchen paper to remove any excess water, then dip them into the batter and gently lower into the hot oil. Fry on a medium heat until golden and just turning brown. Bring out of the oil and place on fresh kitchen paper. Repeat this with all the banana blossom and batter, then season the fried 'fish' with salt just before serving.

For the minted pea purée

Sweat the diced shallot over a low heat in the olive oil until soft and translucent, but do not brown as it will overpower the pea and mint flavours. Add the frozen peas, milk and some salt to taste, then simmer gently for 8 minutes.

Drain off the milk and set it aside. Add the pea mixture and fresh mint leaves to a blender with a little of the reserved milk. Blend until you have a chunky thick purée, adding a little more milk until you get the desired consistency. Taste and season the pea purée, then serve immediately or transfer it straight to the fridge to cool and preserve its colour.

TWICE-COOKED CHIPS

Preparation time: 10 minutes (depending on how many chips you are making)
Cooking time: 50-60 minutes, plus frying time
Serves however many you need
Gluten-free

This recipe was brought in by our previous head chef George, who introduced many good ideas. Strictly speaking, they are more like confit potatoes than chips, but either way this one is a damn fine recipe. The results are worth the effort; they will probably be the best chips you've ever tasted!

King Edward potatoes

Oil (something neutral like grapeseed or rapeseed oil is good)

Sea salt

You will need a fair amount of oil for this recipe as well as a deep roasting tin so you can cover the potatoes completely. Preheat your oven to 170°c.

Peel and rinse the potatoes, then place them into the deep roasting tin, leaving them whole. Pour over the oil until the potatoes are just covered. Your tin should be deep enough that the oil does not come to the top; there should be a little space for when the oil heats, expands, bubbles and works its magic.

Place the tin on a large baking tray and sit that on the bottom shelf of the preheated oven. Leave the potatoes to cook in the oil for 50 minutes to 1 hour. The cooking time will depend on the size of your potatoes; the larger the potatoes are, the longer they will take to cook. Test the potatoes after about 40 minutes with a thin sharp knife (be careful with the very hot oil!). When they are tender right through to the centre, remove the tray from the oven and place on a heatproof mat or board.

Leave the potatoes to cool in the oil, then transfer them to a colander with tongs to drain. When all the oil has dripped off, place the potatoes in a tub and chill in the fridge.

Meanwhile, heat a deep pan of oil to 180°c. If you do not have a thermometer, drop in a small piece of bread to see whether it rises and bubbles quickly. If so, the oil is ready. Cut the chilled potatoes fairly thickly and fry in batches until golden on the outside. Remove the chips from the fryer carefully with a slotted spoon and place on kitchen paper to drain off any excess oil. Season with sea salt before serving.

CHANA MASALA

Preparation time: 10 minutes
Cooking time: 30 minutes
Serves 4
Gluten-free

I just love chana masala; I could eat it every day. I learnt this recipe from the head chef, Shamim, at an Indian restaurant group I used to manage in New Zealand. Making the chole masala spice blend yourself is well worth the effort, but you can pick some up from your favourite online retailer instead. If you cannot find or make any chole masala, bump up the other spices just a little.

30g ginger, peeled

3 cloves of garlic, peeled

2 green chillies (more if you like it spicier)

1 large cinnamon stick

1 tablespoon tomato purée

2 tomatoes, deseeded and finely chopped

1 tablespoon chole masala
(see page 179)

1 tablespoon ground coriander

1 tablespoon ground cumin

1 teaspoon chilli powder (optional)

1/2 teaspoon ground turmeric

500ml masala gravy (see page 184)

2 tins of chickpeas, drained and rinsed

Salt, to taste

A handful fresh coriander leaves
(optional)

1/2 small red onion, thinly sliced
(optional)

First, make a paste by blending the ginger, garlic and chillies together. Fry this paste in a large pan for a couple of minutes with the cinnamon stick.

Next, add the tomato purée and finely chopped tomatoes. Stir in well and cook for a few minutes. Add all the dry spices and cook gently for a few minutes, stirring regularly so the spices do not burn.

Pour in the masala gravy and chickpeas, then cook on a medium heat for 15 minutes, stirring occasionally. When almost done, taste and season with salt.

Serve the chana masala with basmati rice or traditional tandoori roti and garnish it with some fresh coriander leaves and thinly sliced red onion if you like.

FERMENTED BLACK BEAN STIR FRY

Preparation time: 10 minutes
Cooking time: 15-20 minutes
Serves 4

This is a classic Chinese cooking sauce. Fermented black beans are made from soya beans preserved in salt and should be readily available from any Chinese supermarket.

1 fresh red chilli, finely chopped

2 cloves of garlic, minced

3 tablespoons oil

2 tablespoons fermented black beans

200ml Chinese stock (see page 183)

2 tablespoons light soy sauce

2 tablespoons Shaoxing wine

1 tablespoon sesame oil

1 teaspoon Sichuan pepper

1/2 teaspoon white sugar

1 teaspoon cornflour

2 tablespoons water

1 head of broccoli

1 large green pepper

1 block of tofu, deep fried

Fry the chilli and garlic in the oil for a couple of minutes. Next, add the black beans and fry for another couple of minutes before adding the stock, soy sauce, wine, sesame oil, Sichuan pepper and sugar. Bring the sauce to the boil and simmer for a couple of minutes. Meanwhile, combine the cornflour and water to make a smooth paste. Stir this into the simmering sauce to thicken it.

When your sauce is ready, prepare the vegetables and tofu according to your preference and stir fry them in a little more oil until cooked to your liking. Add a tablespoon of water or Chinese stock every couple of minutes, as this helps the stir fry become less oily.

When the vegetables are cooked, stir in the black bean sauce and serve the stir fry with jasmine rice.

GHORMEH SABZI WITH SAFFRON RICE AND YOGHURT DIP

Preparation time: 20 minutes
Cooking time: 1 hour 30 minutes
Serves 4-6
Gluten-free

This Persian dish, which translates as fried herb stew, is a staple in Iranian cuisine and is always served with rice to offset the strong flavours. It's usually made with lamb, but we like lambs, so we use roasted portobello mushrooms instead. Use kidney beans if you can't find pinto.

4 dried mushrooms

1.5 litres hot stock

6 large portobello mushrooms

50g each fresh flat leaf parsley and coriander

25g fresh chives, chopped

25g fenugreek leaves (fresh if possible, or 15g dried)

25g spinach leaves

1 bunch of spring onions, sliced

2 leeks, finely sliced and rinsed

1 tablespoon tomato purée (optional)

½ teaspoon ground turmeric

1 tin of pinto beans

4 dried limes

Salt and pepper

For the saffron rice

250g white basmati rice

Pinch of saffron threads

1 clove of garlic, peeled

For the yoghurt dip

500g plain vegan yoghurt

100g cucumber

10g fresh mint

20g walnuts

30g raisins

1 tablespoon dried rose petals, for garnish (optional)

Preheat the oven to 180°c and soak the dried mushrooms in the hot stock. Clean and quarter the portobello mushrooms, removing the stems. Drizzle generously with olive oil and roast in the oven for 25 minutes. Meanwhile, pick the parsley and coriander leaves off the stalks and put them in a bowl of cold water with the chives, fenugreek leaves if fresh, spinach and spring onions.

Heat some olive oil in a large pan and sauté the leeks gently for 5 minutes until they start to soften. If using, add the tomato purée and cook for 2 minutes. Drain the herbs and vegetables in a colander, then add them to the pan with the turmeric. Cook gently for 10 minutes, or until they start to change colour. Next add the pinto beans, dried limes and stock (dried mushrooms removed).

Season the stew with salt and pepper, then cover with a lid and cook on a low heat, stirring occasionally. After 1 hour, stir in the roasted portobello mushrooms and any juices from the roasting tin, then cook for a further 15 minutes.

For the saffron rice

While the stew is cooking, wash the rice until the water runs clear and then drain in a sieve. Soak the saffron threads in a little hot water. Heat a little olive oil in a pan with a tight-fitting lid, then gently fry the garlic clove for 1 minute. Stir in the rice and fry for another minute until coated in oil.

Cover the rice with water and gently bring to the boil with the lid on (this takes about 10 minutes). As soon as the water starts to boil, stir in the soaked saffron and reduce the heat to its lowest setting. Stir and replace the lid. Cook until all the water has evaporated, then stir once more and replace the lid. Leave off the heat for another 10 minutes. Fluff the rice with a fork before serving.

For the yoghurt dip

Peel, deseed and grate the cucumber. Finely chop the mint, walnuts and raisins. Combine all the ingredients in a serving bowl. Taste and season with a little salt as needed, then garnish with the rose petals if using.

When everything is ready, taste the stew to check the seasoning, then serve it with the saffron rice and yoghurt dip alongside.

GENERAL TSO'S STIR FRY

Preparation time: 15 minutes
Cooking time: 10 minutes
Serves 4
Gluten-free

The origins of this dish are disputed, though the generally accepted version is that it is named after a fictional Chinese general. It has a sweet sauce with flavours of sherry, lemon and ginger which is delicious regardless of where it came from! Easy to make and a real staff favourite.

25g peeled fresh ginger

25g peeled fresh garlic

1 red chilli, deseeded

Sunflower oil

250ml Chinese stock (preferably homemade, see page 183)

3 tablespoons soy sauce
(or 2 tablespoons tamari if you want it to be gluten-free)

3 tablespoons white sugar

2 tablespoons sherry

1½ tablespoons white wine vinegar

30ml lemon juice

15g arrowroot powder

1 large red pepper, deseeded and sliced

1 head of broccoli, cut into small florets

100g baby corn, halved lengthways

300g tofu, deep fried

First, make the sauce. Place the ginger, garlic and chilli in a food processor and blend until very finely chopped. Heat a little sunflower oil in a saucepan and fry this paste for 3 minutes. Next, add the stock, soy sauce, sugar, sherry, vinegar and lemon juice to the pan and bring to the boil. Leave it to simmer for a couple of minutes while you mix the arrowroot with a little cold water to make a paste. Add this paste to the simmering liquid, stirring continuously. This is your sauce.

Put a couple of tablespoons of sunflower oil into a wok over a high heat, then stir fry the vegetables and deep fried tofu. As they cook, splash in a very small amount of water. This will partly steam the stir fry instead of making it too oily. When the vegetables are cooked (this should take approximately 5 minutes) add enough of the sauce to just cover the vegetables.

Serve the tofu and vegetable stir fry with some Chinese sticky rice.

GNOCCHI ARRABBIATA WITH ROASTED ARTICHOKES & SPINACH

Preparation time: 25 minutes, plus 1 hour marinating
Cooking time: 40 minutes
Serves 4

Arrabbiata, a tomato sauce with a hint of chilli, translates as 'angry' in Italian. Traditionally, it's served with penne pasta but gnocchi are a great pairing and much easier to make than you would think. Two chef's tips here: if you have a good independent vegetable supplier, ask them to get you some of last season's potatoes as they have less water content, perfect for gnocchi. Secondly, use chopped tinned tomatoes instead of whole because they have had most of the seeds removed.

For the roasted artichokes

400g tinned artichoke hearts

50ml white wine

A few sprigs of fresh thyme

Salt and pepper, to taste

Olive oil

For the arrabbiata sauce

2 shallots, finely diced

1 red chilli, finely chopped

$1/2$ teaspoon chilli flakes

1 teaspoon smoked paprika

Sprig of fresh thyme

1 teaspoon white sugar

50ml red wine vinegar

3 cloves of garlic, minced

2 tins of good quality chopped tomatoes (preferably San Marzano)

1 bay leaf

Fresh flat leaf parsley, to garnish

For the gnocchi

500g floury potatoes (Desiree or Maris Piper work well)

175g '00' flour

To serve

Handful of baby leaf spinach

Brazil nut 'parmesan' (see page 126)

For the roasted artichokes

Drain and rinse the artichoke hearts, then chop into quarters and combine with the wine, thyme, salt and pepper. Marinate for 1 hour. Preheat the oven to 190°c. Drain off excess liquid from the marinated artichokes and roast them in a little olive oil until they start to colour (about 30 minutes).

For the arrabbiata sauce

Heat some olive oil in a heavy-bottomed pan over a medium heat, then add the shallots and chilli. Sweat them down until soft and translucent before stirring in the chilli flakes, smoked paprika and thyme. Cook for a further minute before adding the sugar and red wine vinegar, then reduce. Now stir in the minced garlic, chopped tomatoes and bay leaf. Cook on a very gentle simmer and reduce the sauce for 20 minutes until it thickens, then taste and season with salt and pepper.

For the gnocchi

Cook the potatoes in boiling salted water (it should taste like sea water) for 40 minutes, or until tender when pierced with a thin sharp knife. Drain and peel the potatoes while hot, then press them through a potato ricer over a clean work surface. Alternatively, thoroughly mash them with a potato masher and then a fork.

Sieve the flour onto the mashed potatoes. With a large knife or dough scraper, cut through the flour to mix it in until a rough dough is formed. It should be firm to the eye, soft to the touch and a little bit sticky (if too sticky, add a little more flour). Roll the dough into a cylinder, cover with a tea towel and leave to rest for 15 minutes.

Dust some flour onto the work surface and roll half of the rested dough into a 2cm thick sausage. Cut this into 3 by 2cm pieces. To shape the gnocchi, roll each individual piece of dough from corner to corner on a gnocchi board (a grooved miniature wooden board) or the prongs of a fork. This creates the classic grooved shape, which helps the sauce stick.

To cook the gnocchi, simply plunge them into a pan of boiling salted water and cook until they rise to the surface, which should only take 1 to 2 minutes.

To serve

Stir the cooked gnocchi into the arrabbiata sauce. Wilt the spinach in a pan and toss it with the roasted artichokes. Divide between bowls and sprinkle with some Brazil nut 'parmesan' if you like.

KORMA

Preparation time: 30 minutes, plus 30
minutes soaking
Cooking time: 40 minutes
Serves 4-6
Gluten-free

This sweet almond and coconut curry is delicious and easy to make once your masala gravy is prepared in advance. My chef's tip here is to buy fresh curry leaves and keep them in the freezer. They can be cooked from frozen and are far superior to the dried ones.

50g cashews

25g oil

4 cardamom pods

1 cinnamon stick

8 curry leaves

100g garlic and ginger paste
(see page 178)

3 tablespoons white sugar

50g ground almonds

800ml masala gravy (see page 184)

300ml coconut milk

20g coconut flour

2 teaspoons salt

1 teaspoon garam masala

1 teaspoon rosewater (optional)

To serve

Cooked vegetables or pulses of your choice

Steamed basmati rice

Poppadoms

Chutney

First, soak the cashews in a bowl of water for 30 minutes. Drain and rinse, then blend in a food processor with a little fresh water to make a cashew paste. Set aside.

Heat the oil over a medium-high heat. When visibly hot, add the cardamom pods and cinnamon stick. Sizzle for about 30 seconds and then add the curry leaves. Stir in the garlic and ginger paste and then the sugar, ground almonds and raw cashew paste.

The pan will be quite hot at this point, so add roughly half of your masala gravy to cool it down and cook until it forms a thick paste. Add the rest of the masala gravy and the coconut milk, then let the sauce simmer gently for 30 minutes. If you would the korma to be less coconutty, leave out some of the coconut milk and add the same amount of plant-based cream once the sauce has simmered.

Meanwhile, boil any vegetables you are using in a pan of salted water with half a teaspoon of turmeric. Drain them in a colander when they are tender.

Just before the sauce has finished simmering, stir in the coconut flour, salt, garam masala and rosewater if using. If you are using any plant-based cream, swirl it through the sauce now.

To serve

Fry the cooked vegetables or pulses (such as chickpeas) of your choice (cauliflower and potatoes are always a good start with korma, but you can use anything you want) in a little oil for a couple of minutes, then pour the desired amount of sauce into the pan with them. Simmer for a couple of minutes before serving your korma with rice, poppadoms and a chutney of your choice.

MEZZE PLATE

You'll find the recipes for the falafel, hummus, harissa and pitta bread shown here on the following pages, as well as the pickled chillies below. Our mezze plate also includes a quinoa tabbouleh, tahini sauce and macadamia feta which you can find the recipes for on pages 62, 168 and 130 respectively.

PICKLED GREEN CHILLIES

Preparation time: 10 minutes
Cooking time: 10 minutes
Makes 1 large jar
Gluten-free

These make a lovely accompaniment to many dishes, especially a mezze. The pickling process is very simple and they keep for ages.

750ml water

750ml white vinegar

3 tablespoons white sugar

3 tablespoons fine sea salt

3 fresh bay leaves

3 cloves of garlic

3 tablespoons coriander seeds (optional)

300g long green mild chillies

Add all the ingredients except the chillies to a saucepan and simmer gently for 10 minutes. Meanwhile, prick each chilli a few times with the point of a small sharp knife, as this helps the chillies absorb the brine more effectively.

Put the chillies upright in a large sterilised jar and pour in the brine. Leave them to sit uncovered for 10 minutes before sealing the lid of the jar. They should keep for weeks like this. You could also slice the chillies and use the same method of pickling if preferred.

PITTA BREAD

Preparation time: 2 hours 30 minutes
Cooking time: 5 minutes
Serves 8-10

This recipe is so satisfying: who doesn't love fresh bread straight out of the oven? Open the pittas to create pockets while they are still warm and stuff them with fresh hummus, falafel, pickles and salad (see the recipes on pages 98, 96 and 92).

1kg plain flour

10g dried yeast

3 teaspoons white sugar

2 teaspoons salt

1 teaspoon baking powder

600g water

A little olive oil

Mix all the ingredients except the oil together by hand in a large bowl, then knead the dough for about 4 minutes on a clean surface. You can use a stand mixer with a dough hook if you like. Wipe a little oil around the bowl and place the dough in, cover with a plate and leave to rise for 2 hours.

Turn the risen dough onto a floured surface and then roll gently into a log shape before cutting into 150g to 200g pieces. Leave the dough balls to rest for a few minutes, covered with a tea towel.

Meanwhile, preheat your oven to its maximum temperature with the baking tray that you will use to cook the pittas inside, so it gets really hot.

Roll each portion of dough into a roughly circular shape with a little flour. Lay the pittas carefully onto the hot baking tray and place in the preheated oven to bake for 5 minutes.

Remove the pittas from the oven and leave them to sit for 3 minutes before serving.

AUTHENTIC FALAFEL

Preparation time: 15 minutes, plus soaking overnight
Cooking time: 15 minutes
Serves 12
Gluten-free

The important thing to remember about falafel is that you do not make them with pre-cooked chickpeas! Fava beans are best if you can get hold of them, otherwise you'll need to buy dried chickpeas and follow the method below for preparing them.

200g dried chickpeas and 200g dried fava beans

1 teaspoon bicarbonate of soda

20g flat leaf parsley

10g fresh coriander

2 tablespoons ground coriander

2 tablespoons ground cumin

2 tablespoons ground black pepper

6 cloves of garlic, finely chopped

8 spring onions, chopped

2 tablespoons toasted sesame seeds

1 teaspoon baking powder

Oil, for deep frying

Place the dried chickpeas and fava beans in a large bowl, add the bicarbonate of soda and give them a stir. Cover with plenty of water and leave to soak overnight. Sometimes organic chickpeas can be quite small and hard, so leaving them a little longer will help.

When the chickpeas and fava beans have been soaked long enough, drain them in a colander and pat them dry with kitchen paper to remove any excess water. Transfer them into a food processor and add the herbs, spices, garlic and spring onions. Blend until the mixture forms a coarse paste. Transfer this mixture to an airtight container and refrigerate for an hour or so.

If your sesame seeds aren't already toasted, you can now heat them in a dry frying pan until golden.

When the falafel mixture is ready, heat the oil in a deep fat fryer or large pot to 180°c. Just before you are ready to start frying, stir the toasted sesame seeds and baking powder into the falafel mixture, then form small patties using roughly a tablespoon for each one.

Carefully place the falafel into the fryer a few at a time and fry for a couple of minutes until they are brown. Remove carefully from the fryer and dry on kitchen paper to remove any residual oil. Serve as part of a mezze plate, in a wrap or however you like them.

HUMMUS
(LIKE A PRO)

Preparation time: 15 minutes, plus soaking overnight
Cooking time: 45 minutes
Makes 1 litre
Gluten-free

All hummus is not created equal sadly; the little plastic pots you buy in the supermarket are mainly water, completely lacking in flavour and texture. This recipe is worth the extra effort, especially if you buy the best tahini you can find, not the dark unhulled stuff. It makes about a litre of hummus but freezes well: just defrost and stir in your olive oil to serve.

300g dried chickpeas

1 teaspoon bicarbonate of soda

1 tablespoon salt

Large pinch of cumin

1 clove of garlic

120g tahini

25ml lemon juice

2 ice cubes

Really good olive oil, to serve

Place the dried chickpeas in a large bowl, add the bicarbonate of soda and give them a stir. Cover the chickpeas with plenty of water and leave to soak overnight. Sometimes organic chickpeas can be quite small and hard, so leaving them a little longer will help.

When the chickpeas have been soaked long enough, drain them in a colander and rinse under fresh water. Put the chickpeas into a large cooking pot, then add plenty of water (enough to cover them completely) with the salt and cumin. Use a big enough pot to allow space for the chickpeas to expand while they cook without overflowing. Bring the chickpeas to the boil and reduce the heat to a gentle simmer.

While the chickpeas are cooking, remove any skins that float to the surface. Cook until slightly overdone. When cooked, keep a little of the water for thinning the hummus later. Drain the cooked chickpeas in the colander and remove as many skins as you can. This is worth the effort as it will make your hummus much smoother and creamier.

While the chickpeas are cooking, put the garlic, tahini and lemon juice into a blender. Blend the mixture until smooth, then transfer to a bowl and set aside.

Put the skinned chickpeas in the blender while they are still warm. Add the ice cubes (they help to keep the hummus aerated) and blend until very smooth, cleaning the sides with a spatula if necessary. Now add the tahini mixture to the puréed chickpeas and blend again, adding some of the chickpea cooking water if necessary to get a really smooth consistency.

Serve the hummus on a plate with a small well in the centre and finish with a generous drizzle of your best olive oil.

ROSE HARISSA

Preparation time: 20 minutes
Cooking time: 40 minutes
Serves plenty!
Gluten-free

Harissa is a fiery North African spice paste usually made from peppers, chillies, garlic, caraway seeds, cumin and coriander. It's great for pepping up many dishes: add some to a plain soup, brush over vegetables before roasting or just use as a spicy accompaniment. This version includes rosewater which gives the harissa a sweet, perfumed aroma and just a little more personality.

500g red peppers

3 dried red chillies (Kashmiri are good)

4 cloves of garlic

1 teaspoon caraway seeds

1 tablespoon coriander seeds

1 tablespoon dried rose petals

1 teaspoon granulated sugar

1 teaspoon salt

125ml olive oil

4 tablespoons red wine vinegar

2 tablespoons fresh lemon juice

1 tablespoon tomato purée

1 tablespoon rosewater

Preheat your oven to 170°c. Halve the peppers lengthways and deseed them. Halve the pieces lengthways again and place them on a baking tray. Brush with a little olive oil, then roast the peppers in the preheated oven for about 40 minutes or until they start to blister. Don't let them blacken because the burnt flavour will dominate the harissa. When the peppers have started to blister, transfer them to a bowl and cover with cling film. Leave them to steam for 10 minutes and cool slightly, then you should be able to peel off the skins quite easily. Dice the prepared pepper.

While the peppers are in the oven, cut the stalks off the dried chillies and slice them lengthways. If you would prefer the harissa less spicy, remove the seeds by scraping them out with the back of a knife. Soak the chillies in hot water for 30 minutes, then slice them up with a sharp knife.

Heat a little of the olive oil in a pan and add the garlic, caraway and coriander seeds. Fry for 2 minutes to release the aromas before transferring the mixture to a food processor. Add the diced pepper, sliced chillies, rose petals, sugar and salt to the processor and pulse a few times until combined. Stir in the remaining ingredients, then transfer the harissa to a sterilised airtight jar. If you top this with more olive oil it will keep in the fridge for weeks.

MUSHROOM RAGOUT WITH FRIED POLENTA, ONIONS & CAVOLO NERO

Preparation time: 15 minutes, plus setting and soaking time
Cooking time: 30 minutes
Serves 4
Gluten-free when you omit the onions

This recipe has been a favourite of nearly all our chefs when we had it on the menu; there were no objections to this being served if there was any left at the end of a shift. If you haven't made any of the demi-glace previously, you can substitute it with a shop-bought gravy, made slightly stronger.

For the mushroom ragout

500g mixed mushrooms (such as chestnut, oyster and king oyster)

4 shallots, sliced

2 cloves of garlic

2 sprigs of fresh thyme

300ml hot fresh stock (homemade is best)

200ml coconut milk

6 tablespoons demi-glace
(see page 182)

6 tablespoons nutritional yeast flakes

4 tablespoons finely diced chives

Salt and pepper, to taste

25g arrowroot powder

For the fried polenta

1 litre water

25g vegan stock powder

250g polenta

10g chives, finely chopped

Vegetable oil, for deep frying

For the crispy onions

1 large onion, thinly sliced

500ml soya milk

150g plain flour

2 teaspoons onion powder

1 teaspoon each paprika and salt

To serve

A few handfuls of cavolo nero, washed and sliced

For the mushroom ragout

Cut the mushrooms into evenly sized pieces (not too small; this dish is great with a bit of texture to it) and gently heat a little olive oil in a frying pan. Fry the sliced shallots gently until they are soft, then add the garlic, thyme and mushrooms. Cook for a few minutes until the mushrooms release their liquid, then add the hot stock and coconut milk. Cook for 5 minutes before stirring in the demi-glace, nutritional yeast and chives. Season to taste with salt and a good twist of black pepper. Mix the arrowroot with a little cold water to make a smooth paste, then add this to the ragout and stir constantly until the sauce has thickened slightly. Leave on a low heat until ready to serve.

For the fried polenta

Line a 23cm square baking tray with greaseproof paper. Bring the water and stock to the boil in a saucepan, then pour in the polenta and whisk continuously to avoid any lumps forming. After about 2 minutes, stir in the chopped chives and some black pepper to taste. Pour the polenta quickly into the prepared baking tray and smooth out with a spatula. To get a really flat surface, cover the hot polenta with another piece of baking paper and a tea towel so you can smooth it out. Leave the polenta to cool in the fridge until it has set before cutting into triangles. Heat a saucepan of oil and check the temperature by adding a small cube of bread; if it floats to the surface and bubbles then the oil is ready. Deep fry the polenta triangles in the hot oil until slightly golden at the edges. This should take about 3 to 4 minutes. Alternatively, you can shallow fry the polenta triangles and flip them over halfway through the cooking time.

For the crispy onions

Soak the sliced onion in the soya milk, making sure it is fully submerged, for 1 hour. Drain the soaked onion in a colander. Mix the flour and seasonings together, use this to coat the sliced onion and deep fry in hot oil until golden and crispy. Drain and cool on kitchen paper before serving.

To serve

Steam the cavolo nero for about 5 minutes, then serve it with the mushroom ragout and fried polenta, topped with the crispy onions.

MUSHROOM, SUN-DRIED TOMATO AND RICE BURGER

Preparation time: 15 minutes, plus 1 hour chilling
Cooking time: 30-35 minutes
Makes 8
Gluten-free when using a gluten-free burger bun

200g organic short grain brown rice

375ml water

200g white mushrooms, sliced

1 onion, diced

30g basil, finely sliced (including stalks)

50g sun-dried tomatoes, soaked and roughly chopped

Salt and pepper

This was on our menu for years, from the day we opened. It's a great base recipe that you can tweak to your heart's content. My suggestions would be to add some chopped black olives, cooked beans or chickpeas to up the protein content. We use brown rice as a binder in the burger to give it firmness and texture and soak up any excess liquid. Too many veggie burgers are just mush in a bun.

Rinse the rice, then transfer it to a large pot with a lid (one that does not have holes in) and pour in the water. This is deliberately slightly less than you would normally use, to give the rice some bite and ensure it can absorb any excess liquid from the mushrooms. Bring the water to the boil, stir the rice and then reduce the heat to a minimum with the lid on. After about 15 minutes, stir the rice again and check to see how far the rice is from being done. Once the water has evaporated, stir once again, turn off the heat, put the lid back on and leave for another 5 minutes. We are aiming for the rice to be just undercooked, with a definite bite.

While the rice is steaming, heat some oil in a wide frying pan. Add the sliced mushrooms, basil stalks and onion and spread them out to cover the base of the pan evenly. Fry on a medium to high heat, stirring occasionally, until all the water has evaporated from the mushrooms and the mixture is starting to brown and stick to the pan. Scrape this brown sticky stuff from the pan with a wooden spoon: it's full of flavour.

Stir the mushroom mixture into the rice along with the sun-dried tomatoes and basil leaves. Season the burger mix with a generous amount of salt and pepper, then transfer it to a food processor and blend until coarse. You should be able to just make out the rice grains, so do not over-blend to a purée but if it is too coarse and the rice grains are whole, the burgers will not hold together as well.

For best results, put the blended burger mix in the fridge and leave to chill for an hour. Roll the burger mix into 100g balls before pressing them into patties, then fry each burger on a medium heat.

To serve the burgers, pick a good quality bun, some vegan mayonnaise (see page 174) and chilli sauce (see page 158), then add your choice of salad and cashew cheese (see page 136). Enjoy.

NOODLE STIR FRY
WITH SATAY SAUCE

Preparation time: 10 minutes

Cooking time: 30 minutes

Serves 4

Gluten-free when using gluten-free noodles

This recipe has been a favourite customer request over the years. It's so quick and easy if you use shop-bought peanut butter, but make sure you do not use the wholefood variety that contains skins, as it can be bitter and does not make good satay. We think roasting your own peanuts is definitely worth the time and effort. The sauce can be eaten hot or cold as a dressing.

For the satay sauce

300g raw peanuts, skins removed

250g coconut milk

200g water

140g lime juice

100g sweet chilli sauce

30g tamari

For the noodles

1 thumb-sized piece of ginger, grated

3 tablespoons soy sauce

1 tablespoon sesame oil

1 teaspoon white sugar

1 red pepper, sliced

1 large carrot, julienned

100g baby corn, sliced lengthways

100g mangetout, sliced lengthways

Your favourite noodles

Spring onions, sliced

Chilli flakes (optional)

For the satay sauce

Preheat the oven to 160°c and then roast the peanuts slowly on a baking tray for about 20 minutes, checking them every 5 minutes. You want the peanuts to be evenly golden and not too dark.

Put the roasted peanuts and all the remaining ingredients into a food processor and blend until the sauce is almost smooth but still has a little texture. You can now heat the sauce gently in a pan if serving hot. It will thicken quite quickly when heated, so adjust with water or more lime juice and coconut milk if needed to achieve your desired consistency.

For the noodles

Bring a large pot of salted water to the boil and heat a wok or frying pan. Meanwhile, combine the grated ginger, soy sauce, sesame oil and sugar in a bowl.

Stir fry all the vegetables except the spring onions with a little oil in the hot pan over a high heat. At the same time, cook the noodles in the boiling water according to the packet instructions.

After a few minutes of stir frying the vegetables, stir in the ginger and soy mixture. Now transfer the cooked noodles and a couple of spoonfuls of the cooking water to the vegetables. Mix well and immediately serve in bowls, topped with the warm satay sauce and garnished with sliced spring onion and chilli flakes if using.

RIBOLLITA

Preparation time: 20 minutes
Cooking time: 1 hour 30 minutes
Serves 4

Ribollita is a classic hearty rustic soup from Tuscany using cannellini beans, cavolo nero and stale bread. It tastes better if you leave it for a few days to let the flavours develop, so make a huge batch and eat it for most of the week.

For the beans

150g dried cannellini beans, soaked in water overnight

4 whole cloves of garlic, peeled and bashed slightly

1 large shallot, sliced

2 fresh bay leaves

2 sprigs of thyme

1.5 litres vegetable stock

For the ribollita

Olive oil

1 teaspoon fennel seeds

2 large shallots, sliced

3 cloves of garlic, sliced

1 large carrot, peeled and diced into 1cm cubes

2 sticks of celery, sliced or 1/2 a bulb of fennel

1 sprig of rosemary

6 ripe plum tomatoes, diced

2 medium potatoes, peeled and cut into 2cm cubes

5 leaves of cavolo nero or savoy cabbage

100g stale white bread such as ciabatta or baguette, cut into 2cm cubes

Salt and pepper, to taste

For the beans

Drain the soaked cannellini beans and put them in a large pot with the garlic, shallot, bay leaves, thyme and just enough vegetable stock to cover everything by about 5cm. Cook the beans in this broth for 45 minutes, skimming off any debris that floats to the surface. When the beans are just a little more than al dente (not quite cooked) remove them from the heat, drain and reserve the cooking liquid for later.

For the ribollita

Place a large heavy-bottomed saucepan on a medium heat and add a good splash of olive oil with the fennel seeds. Stir for a minute before adding the shallots, garlic, carrot, celery or fennel and rosemary. Fry gently for 5 minutes but do not brown. Add the plum tomatoes and cook for another 3 minutes. Next, add the cooked beans and their reserved cooking liquid. Simmer for 30 minutes, adding a little water from time to time if necessary.

Now add the potato and cook for 10 minutes before adding the cavolo nero and bread. Cook until the potatoes are tender, which should take about 15 to 20 minutes depending on what type of potatoes are used. Add a little extra water or stock if you would like the soup to be a little thinner, noting that it will thicken slightly when it cools.

Taste the ribollita and season with salt and pepper. For the best results, chill overnight before reheating and serve by finishing with an excellent olive oil and some really good quality Italian bread.

SEITAN STEAK WITH HASSELBACK POTATOES

Preparation time: 20 minutes
Cooking time: 1 hour
Serves 4

Seitan (or wheat gluten) has been eaten in China since the 6th century, and has been adopted in the western world for the last 50 years as a meat substitute. It is made by washing wheat flour dough with water until all the starch granules have been removed, leaving the sticky insoluble gluten as an elastic mass, which is then cooked before being eaten. We make the dough here by using gluten flour and simmering it in a flavoured stock.

For the cooking liquid

1.5 litres vegetable stock

100ml soy sauce

50ml sherry

20g dried mushrooms

2 tablespoons maple syrup

1 tablespoon tomato purée

For the dough

200g gluten flour

50g chickpea flour

2 tablespoons salt

1 tablespoon onion powder

1 teaspoon garlic powder

1/2 teaspoon paprika

300ml water

For the Hasselback potatoes

4 medium-size potatoes

A few sprigs of fresh rosemary

Olive oil

Salt and pepper

To serve

Peppercorn sauce (see page 164)

Tenderstem broccoli

For the cooking liquid

Put all the ingredients into a medium-size saucepan and bring to the boil. While this is heating up you can make the seitan dough.

For the dough

Combine all the dry ingredients before adding the water. Mix with your hands first for a minute or two, then turn out the dough on a clean surface or board and knead again for a couple of minutes until soft. Cut the dough into quarters and place the pieces in the hot cooking liquid. Make sure they are all fully submerged, cover the pan with a lid and simmer for 40 minutes. The dough will expand a lot as it absorbs some of the liquid.

After 40 minutes, check the centre of each piece to make sure that the seitan is cooked right through. Remove all the dough pieces and leave them to cool. Carve into thick slices for this recipe.

To fry the seitan steaks, use a good few tablespoons of olive oil in the pan and cook on a medium heat. If the heat is too high, the seitan will go crispy.

For the Hasselback potatoes

You can make these while the seitan is simmering. Preheat the oven to 200°c. Scrub the potatoes clean and pat them dry. Use a sharp knife to cut slits in the potatoes along their width, going most of the way through but not completely so they remain whole. Each cut should be about 2mm apart. A little tip here is to lay each potato in between the handles of 2 wooden spoons so you do not cut all the way through. Place the potatoes on a baking tray and rub with olive oil, salt and pepper. Tear the rosemary into smaller sprigs and tuck these into the slits. Roast in the preheated oven for 30 minutes, then check they are starting to crisp up, brush on another layer of oil and roast for a further 20 to 30 minutes.

To serve

Serve the Hasselback potatoes straight from the oven with the seitan steaks, peppercorn sauce and some lightly steamed tenderstem broccoli seasoned with salt and your best olive oil.

SORREL RISOTTO

Preparation time: 5 minutes
Cooking time: 30 minutes
Serves 4
Gluten-free

Sorrel is an under-used leaf which has a lovely lemon flavour. This super simple risotto is so tasty. A few wild garlic leaves, sliced and stirred into this, are a lovely addition when they're in season.

2 large shallots

Good olive oil

2 litres good vegetable stock

350g carnaroli risotto rice

200g sorrel leaves, washed and sliced

Salt, to taste

40ml oat cream

25ml lemon juice

1 tablespoon nutritional yeast flakes

First, finely slice the shallots and fry them gently in some olive oil on a low to medium heat until soft and translucent. While this is happening, heat up the stock and make sure it's hot.

Next, add the rice to the shallot pan and stir to coat the grains in oil. Continue to stir until the rice gets hot, checking with the back of your fingers. You want to get the rice too hot to hold. This is the time to add half of the hot stock and keep stirring.

When the first batch of stock has absorbed, add a ladleful at a time and stir until absorbed. Repeat this process for 5 minutes before adding the sorrel leaves. Stir in a little salt here as it will help keep the rice slightly firm on the outside. Keep adding a little stock at a time until the rice has cooked.

Finally, mix the oat cream, lemon juice and nutritional yeast together in a small jug. Stir until the mixture is smooth, pour into the risotto and then season to taste.

Serve the risotto with a good twist of black pepper and some grated vegan cheese on top if you like.

Salads

RAW 'NOODLE' SALAD

Preparation time: 15 minutes

Serves 4

Gluten-free

For this simple salad, you can use a spiraliser to create noodle-shaped vegetables or use a peeler to cut them into a pappardelle shape (long wide strips).

2 courgettes

2 large carrots

1 sweet potato, peeled

1 red pepper

1 bunch of spring onions

100g baby corn

For the sesame dressing

Juice of 1 large or 2 small limes

2 tablespoons red wine vinegar

2 tablespoons white wine vinegar

2 tablespoons sesame oil

2 tablespoons tamari

1 tablespoon olive oil

1 tablespoon brown sugar

20g fresh ginger, peeled

2 spring onions, chopped

1 red chilli, deseeded if preferred

1 clove of garlic, peeled

Salt and pepper

Prepare the courgettes, carrots and sweet potato either with your spiraliser or peeler, creating noodle-like strands or long wide strips as preferred. Thinly slice the red pepper and spring onions, then halve or quarter the baby corn lengthways.

Place all the dressing ingredients in a blender and blend on a high speed for 2 minutes. Taste to check the seasoning, adding more salt and pepper if necessary.

Mix all the prepared ingredients together and toss with the sesame dressing to suit your taste.

RAW WALNUT
COURGETTI BOLOGNESE

Preparation time: 20 minutes, plus overnight soaking
Serves 4
Gluten-free

This is a popular dish in the café which was developed through us mucking around in the kitchen, trying to make a more satiating salad that wasn't too salad-y and was packed full of protein for all the gym goers at the Green Rocket. You will need a spiraliser for this dish.

100g sun-dried tomatoes

100g walnuts

10g dates

1 carrot, chopped

1 stick of celery, chopped

1 sprig of fresh rosemary, finely chopped

1 fresh red chilli (optional)

2 cloves of garlic, peeled

20g fresh basil

30ml olive oil

Salt and pepper, to taste

3 organic courgettes (straight ones are easier to spiralise)

1 punnet of cherry tomatoes, halved

Soak the sun-dried tomatoes, walnuts and dates overnight in separate bowls of water. Drain them the next day, retaining the liquid from the sun-dried tomatoes to use later.

In a food processor, blend the walnuts and dates to a rough consistency and then set this mixture aside. Add all the remaining ingredients except the courgettes and cherry tomatoes to the food processor. Blend until smooth to create a sauce, using a little of the sun-dried tomato soaking liquid to reach a good consistency. Stir the walnut and date paste into the sauce and taste to check the seasoning, adding more salt and pepper if needed.

Spiralise the courgettes to create long spaghetti-like strands. Stir through the desired amount of 'Bolognese' sauce, then add the halved cherry tomatoes.

You could also combine the sauce with other spiralised vegetables, or just use normal cooked spaghetti and warm up the sauce for a healthier take on the classic dish.

RAW PAD THAI SALAD

Preparation time: 15 minutes

Cooking time: 5 minutes (optional)

Serves 4

Gluten-free

This recipe was very similar to a traditional one that I learned to make at cooking school in Thailand, but I switched it up slightly after discovering kelp noodles. They look almost exactly like cooked vermicelli noodles, which are readily available from nearly every supermarket. Use them instead if you cannot wait for the kelp noodles to arrive from your favourite online retailer.

For the salad

75g peanuts

200g kelp noodles

3 shallots, finely sliced

2 large carrots, finely sliced

1/2 daikon radish, finely sliced

4 spring onions, finely sliced

10g coriander leaves

5g chives, finely diced

Chilli flakes, to taste (optional)

Salt, to taste

For the dressing (makes 250ml)

60ml fresh lime juice

30g toasted sesame oil

25g fresh ginger (peeled weight)

25ml tamari

15g tamarind paste

10g agave syrup

1 teaspoon black pepper

1 clove of garlic

If you want to keep this salad 100% raw, do not roast the peanuts, but I feel it tastes better if they are roasted. Place the peanuts on a baking tray lined with greaseproof paper and dry roast in the oven on a low to medium heat for approximately 15 minutes until golden brown.

Meanwhile, make the dressing. Place your blender jug on a set of kitchen scales and weigh in all the ingredients, then blend until there are no lumps of garlic or ginger.

Rinse the kelp noodles and finely sliced shallots under cold running water. Ideally, use a mandoline to slice all the vegetables because it makes them look beautiful. Be careful not to cut yourself though, as they are very sharp. Using a large knife to slice everything is just fine. Grated vegetables are ok as well if you are less fussy about presentation or short on time.

Mix all the salad ingredients together in a bowl. Toss the salad with a generous amount of your dressing (I like to use a lot). Season with salt to taste, then garnish the salad with the roasted or raw peanuts, plus a few extra chives and coriander leaves if you like.

TEMPEH CAESAR SALAD

Preparation time: 15 minutes
Cooking time: 10 minutes
Serves 4

This has all the elements of a classic Caesar salad: fresh lettuce, salty capers, crunchy croutons, savoury tempeh and crispy 'bacon' with a creamy dressing and parmesan-like topping. If you do not have any romaine lettuce available, use 1 baby gem lettuce per person.

1 small ciabatta loaf

Olive oil

Salt and pepper

2 x 250g blocks of tempeh, cubed

2 romaine lettuces, leaves separated

8 sun-dried tomatoes, sliced

4 tablespoons baby capers, rinsed

Coconut bacon (see page 180)

For the Caesar dressing

250g vegan mayonnaise (see page 174)

25g nutritional yeast flakes

20g lemon juice

1/2 teaspoon yeast extract

10g vegan Worcestershire sauce

5g Tabasco

50g soya cream

To serve

Brazil nut parmesan (see page 126)

Preheat the oven to 170°c. Cut the ciabatta into thin slices and coat them with a little olive oil, then season with some salt and pepper. Lay them on a baking tray and bake in the oven on a low shelf until the croutons turn a golden colour, turning occasionally. Leave them to cool.

Fry the tempeh cubes in a good amount of oil so they cook evenly and turn golden. Drain on kitchen paper and season with salt and pepper, then allow to cool.

Meanwhile, combine the romaine lettuce leaves, sun-dried tomatoes, capers, coconut bacon and ciabatta croutons in a large bowl. Add the tempeh once cooled.

For the Caesar dressing

This is so easy to make, tastes great and actually makes salad moreish... simply put all the ingredients in a food processor and blend, blend, blend!

To serve

Pour a generous amount of Caesar dressing over the salad and then toss to mix everything well. Serve in large bowls, garnished with a generous helping of Brazil nut parmesan.

Cheeses

BRAZIL NUT 'PARMESAN'

Preparation time: 5 minutes
Makes approx. 500g
Gluten-free

This is a super simple and tasty garnish that will keep in an airtight container for ages. We use it anywhere you would use parmesan; it's especially great on pasta dishes.

500g Brazil nuts
25g nutritional yeast flakes
7g black salt

Blend all the ingredients together in a food processor until the mixture has a consistency like large grains of sand. Be careful not to over-blend this, otherwise it will become sticky. Serve in any way you would use normal parmesan, over pasta or gnocchi for example.

CASHEW BOURSIN

Preparation time: 10 minutes, plus soaking
overnight
Makes 350-400g
Gluten-free

We have been making this herby cheese since the day we opened our doors in early 2013. I just love nut cheeses as they are rich, indulgent, healthy and really tasty.

275g cashews

25ml lemon juice

20g nutritional yeast flakes

15g flat leaf parsley

10g chives, finely diced

2 tablespoons onion powder

1 tablespoon coconut oil

4 teaspoons sea salt

1 teaspoon garlic powder

1 teaspoon tamari

1 teaspoon black pepper

Soak the cashews in water overnight for a minimum of 12 hours and up to 24. You can speed up this process by boiling them gently and rinsing them well, but soaking overnight is definitely preferable.

Drain the cashews, then blend all the ingredients together in a high-powered food processor until smooth. It should have a spreadable texture and needs to be stored in the fridge.

MACADAMIA FETA

Preparation time: 10 minutes, plus 24 hours
soaking and straining
Cooking time: 30 minutes
Makes about 400g
Gluten-free

You can use a few blanched almonds to make up the 300g of nuts and keep costs down, as macadamias can be very expensive, though the exceptional taste of the macadamias are worth the cost. You will need some cheesecloth for this recipe.

300g macadamia nuts

180ml water

1 tablespoon cider vinegar

1 tablespoon olive oil

2 teaspoons salt

1/2 teaspoon black pepper

Soak the macadamias in water overnight for a minimum of 12 hours and up to 24. Drain and rinse, then put them in a high-powered food processor with all the remaining ingredients. Blend on a low speed, then turn the speed up to high until you have a smooth paste.

Lay a piece of cheesecloth in a bowl, place the macadamia paste on top, tie the cloth at the top with an elastic band to wrap the cheese securely and squeeze out any excess water. Place in a sieve over the bowl and leave to strain in the fridge for 12 hours.

When the cheese has strained, preheat your oven to 175°c. Spread the macadamia mixture out on a baking tray lined with greaseproof paper to form a layer roughly 2.5cm thick. Try to select the right size baking tray here so the paste meets all the edges evenly. If it is uneven, you will get browning at the edges and it won't look as good. Cover the paste with another sheet of baking paper and press with your hands to make it a little firmer.

Bake the cheese in the preheated oven for 30 minutes. Remove from the oven and allow to cool before refrigerating. After it has been in the fridge for an hour or so you can cut the feta into cubes before serving.

MARINATED 'CHEESY' TOFU

Preparation time: 5 minutes
Cooking time: 25 minutes
Serves plenty
Gluten-free

This is one of those strange recipes that is far superior to the sum of its parts. It is no culinary masterpiece by any means, but it is delicious. Serve hot or cold, on a salad instead of halloumi, in a sandwich, or just eat it straight out of the fridge.

100ml olive oil

30ml tamari

2 cloves of garlic

A few flat leaf parsley leaves

1 packet of firm tofu, drained and rinsed

25g nutritional yeast flakes

Preheat the oven to 180°c. Blend the oil, tamari, garlic and parsley together in a blender until the mixture is smooth like a dressing. Alternatively, use the garlic and parsley oil on page 182.

Cut the block of tofu into thick strips just under 1cm each. Place the tofu on a baking tray lined with greaseproof paper. Pour the garlic and parsley oil evenly over each slice of tofu. A chef's tip here is to use the smallest tray possible which will fit the tofu tightly in one layer. This stops the marinade from running off the tofu while it is baking.

Bake the tofu in the preheated oven for about 15 minutes. Remove from the oven and sprinkle half of the yeast flakes on top, then flip the slices over and sprinkle with the remaining flakes. Place the tray back into the oven and bake the 'cheesy' tofu on the middle shelf for 10 minutes.

Serve straight away or refrigerate and then reheat as required in a non-stick pan by quickly searing the slices on each side.

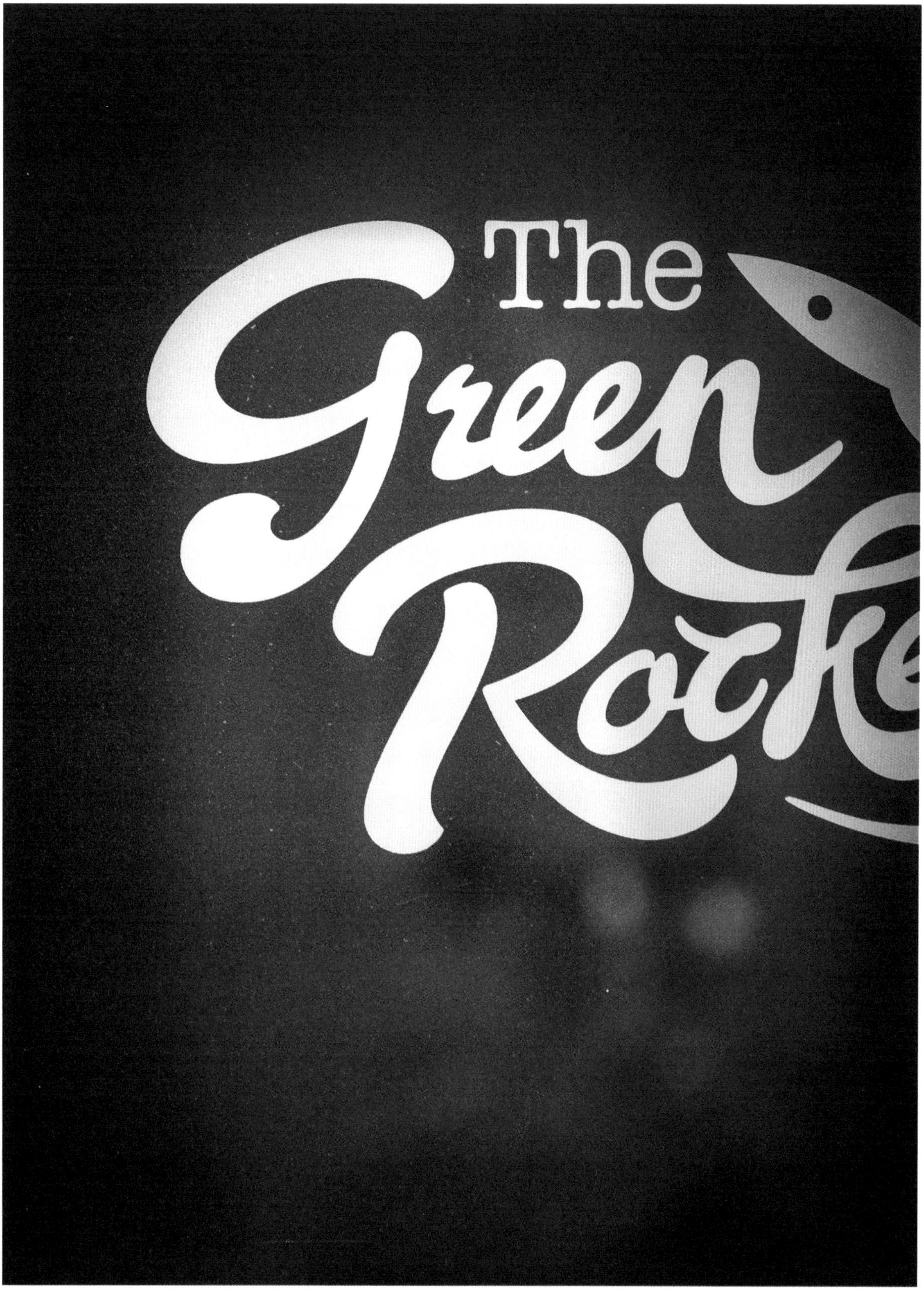
The
Green
Rocke

REJUVELAC

Preparation time: 1 week
Makes approx. 600ml
Gluten-free

Rejuvelac is a prebiotic-rich liquid containing friendly bacteria that are beneficial for gut health, made by fermenting grains. We use quinoa in our recipe to keep it gluten-free, though it can be made with many other grains. You will need some clean muslin cloths and about a week to prepare this, but it's well worth doing.

150g organic quinoa

Sterilise a container that has a flat bottom, using boiling water to clean it. Ideally it should be large enough for you to spread the quinoa in a 0.5cm deep layer. Once you have done this, cover the quinoa with water and place a muslin cloth over the container. Secure the cloth with either a very large elastic band or some masking tape, then leave the quinoa to soak for at least 12 hours.

After the 12 hours have elapsed, drain the quinoa, rinse the grains with cold water and then add just enough fresh water to keep the grains moist but not immersed. The goal is to get the grains to sprout. Cover with some fresh muslin and leave in a warm place out of direct sunlight for 2 days.

During these 2 days, rinse the grains gently to leave them just a little moist twice per day until they have sprouted (you will see a little tail grow on each grain) which should start to happen after approximately 24 hours. Once they have sprouted fully (after 3 or 4 days), rinse one final time and add approximately 600ml of fresh water, cover with fresh muslin once more and leave as it is for 3 days in the warm dark place.

After the 3 days are up, strain the liquid through a fine sieve. It should have a slightly tart, 'cheesy' and lemony flavour. Store the rejuvelac in an airtight container in the fridge for up to 1 month.

STRONG CASHEW CHEESE

Preparation time: 5 minutes, plus soaking
overnight
Makes about 400g
Gluten-free

This is the cheese we currently use most of at the Green Rocket and it's delicious! Making your own rejuvelac (a fermented drink made from sprouted grains) is well worth the effort. You can also break open and add a beta-carotene capsule, which will colour the cheese slightly yellow as well as adding health benefits. Be aware of finding gelatine-free capsules if you do decide to do this.

275g cashews

100ml rejuvelac (see page 134)

15g nutritional yeast flakes

1 tablespoon medium brown miso

1/2 teaspoon salt

Soak the cashews in water overnight for a minimum of 12 hours and up to 24. You can speed up this process by boiling them gently for 20 minutes and rinsing them well, but soaking overnight is definitely preferable.

Drain the cashews, then blend all the ingredients together in a high-powered food processor until smooth. You may need to scrape the sides down and blend again halfway through. It should have a spreadable texture and needs to be stored in the fridge.

CASHEW CREAM

Preparation time: 5 minutes
Makes 75g (4 portions)
Gluten-free

This recipe is simply our strong cashew cheese lengthened with rejuvelac (or a little water and some salt) to make a delicious savoury cream. Great with gnocchi or pasta dishes and useful for adding flavour to white sauces.

50g strong cashew cheese
(see above)

25g rejuvelac (see page 134)

Simply blend the cashew cheese and rejuvelac together in a blender until smooth.

Desserts

APPLE & BERRY CRUMBLE WITH CRÈME ANGLAISE

Preparation time: 20-25 minutes
Cooking time: 30 minutes
Serves 4 (generously)
Gluten-free

The hazelnut crumble topping here is gluten-free and the filling has an unusual touch of lavender that really lifts the fruit and makes this a delicious summery dessert.

For the apple, berry and lavender filling

500g cooking apples, peeled and chopped

500g frozen berries

150g white sugar

40ml white wine

1 small cinnamon stick

A few sprigs of lavender

For the hazelnut crumble topping

150g vegan margarine

150g white sugar

150g ground hazelnuts

150g gluten-free flour

For the crème anglaise

500ml soya milk

2 tablespoons maple syrup

1 teaspoon vanilla paste or 2 vanilla pods, split lengthways with a knife and seeds scraped out

Small pinch of ground turmeric

$1^1/_2$ tablespoons cornflour

For the apple, berry and lavender filling

Combine all the ingredients except the berries and sugar in a saucepan, cook gently until the apples start to break down, then stir in the berries and sugar. You can now transfer the filling to individual ovenproof ramekins or one large dish.

For the hazelnut crumble topping

Preheat your oven to 160°c. Cream the margarine and sugar together with the back of a wooden spoon until the sugar dissolves into the fat and the texture is light and fluffy. Combine the flour and ground hazelnuts, then add this mixture to the creamed margarine and sugar. Stir in a little, then use your fingers to combine the ingredients until the consistency is like breadcrumbs.

Spread the crumble topping onto a baking tray that has been lined with greaseproof paper. Bake in the preheated oven for 20 minutes, stirring every 5 minutes to break up any lumps and ensure it cooks evenly. Repeat until the topping is golden brown and smells fantastic. It will still seem soft after the 20 minutes but when cool it will be crumblier. This keeps very well in an airtight container for a few weeks.

For the crème anglaise

Put three quarters of the milk into a saucepan with the maple syrup, vanilla paste or seeds and turmeric over a low heat. Meanwhile, whisk the remaining milk with the cornflour to make a paste, ensuring there are no lumps. Whisk this paste into the warm milk mixture until it starts to gently steam (do not let it boil). At this point, stop whisking and just stir the custard gently. When it has thickened slightly, take the pan off the heat and use as required.

If you are not serving the crème anglaise straight away, allow it to cool and store in the fridge. It will thicken slightly more when it has been chilled. Reheat gently to serve.

To assemble and serve

Top the filling with the crumble mix and bake in the oven for about 10 minutes. The crumble should have a slight crunch and the fruit underneath should be piping hot. Serve with the warm vegan crème anglaise.

BISCOFF AMARETTO TIRAMISU

Preparation time: 1 hour, plus soaking overnight

Serves 8

You can make this in a 9 inch/23cm springform cake tin, though we use 250ml Kilner jars for individual servings which adds a real sense of occasion to this moreish dessert. Although the recipe seems complicated, it's pretty straightforward once you've done it once and to save time you can make them in batches as they freeze well.

For the first and third layers

Lotus Biscoff biscuits

3 teaspoons instant coffee

3 tablespoons amaretto

100ml boiling water

For the second layer

350g silken tofu, drained and dried

125g vegan dark chocolate, melted

3 tablespoons amaretto

1$1/2$ tablespoons agave or maple syrup

For the fourth layer

250g raw cashews, soaked in water overnight

150ml cold water

3 tablespoons agave or maple syrup

2$1/2$ teaspoons vanilla extract

2 teaspoons nutritional yeast flakes

$1/2$ teaspoon coffee granules

2 teaspoons agar powder

150ml boiling water

Cocoa powder, to finish

For the first and third layers

Use the quantities given above for each of the two Biscoff layers, using as many biscuits as you need to create a complete layer each time. Whisk the coffee and amaretto into the boiling water, then pour the liquid into a shallow bowl. Soak each biscuit briefly on both sides, then place them into the tin or jars (breaking them up to fit if using jars). Be careful not to oversaturate the biscuits in the liquid, as they will fall apart once they get too soggy. Do this carefully until you have completely covered the base of the tin or jar (or the second layer), overlapping the biscuits so there are no gaps. Smooth out the surface using the back of a teaspoon to create an even layer.

For the second layer

Place all the ingredients into a food processor and blend until the mixture is very thick and creamy. Spoon this onto the coffee biscuit base, but don't apply any pressure as it's all very delicate. Place the tin or jars in the freezer for 30 minutes before attempting the third layer, which is identical to the first layer, so follow the instructions above once the tofu layer is hard enough.

For the fourth layer

Drain the soaked cashews, then place them in a high-powered food processor with the cold water, maple syrup, vanilla, nutritional yeast and coffee. Blend until the mixture is totally smooth, which may take several minutes, and scrape down the sides of the processor with a plastic spatula halfway through to incorporate everything. Meanwhile, mix the agar into the boiling water until thoroughly combined. Add this thickening agent to the mixture in the processor and blend for another minute. The cashew cream should now be ready for pouring.

Take the tin or jars containing the first three layers out of the fridge and make sure they have set slightly before carefully spooning the cashew cream on top. Smooth it out with the back of a spoon, then place the tiramisu in the freezer for 1 hour. Transfer it to the fridge after this time and leave to set overnight. To serve, dust the top generously with cocoa powder.

CHOCOLATE HAZELNUT BISCOTTI

Preparation time: 15 minutes
Cooking time: 50 minutes
Makes enough to fill a 2 litre container

These hard Italian biscuits are ideal for dunking in coffee or a nice dessert wine. Biscotti means twice baked, but you can just bake them once for a softer, more cookie-like biscuit which is also delicious.

50g hazelnuts

125g coconut oil

150g white sugar

120g liquid egg replacement (we use Crackd)

1 teaspoon vanilla paste

300g plain flour

1½ teaspoons baking powder

1 teaspoon cocoa powder

¼ teaspoon salt

100g chocolate chips (or a block of chocolate, cut into shards)

Preheat your oven to 170°c and roast the hazelnuts on a baking tray for approximately 20 minutes or until they start to turn golden and the dark skin flakes off easily. To remove the skins, place the hazelnuts in a clean tea towel and rub until all of the dark skin has been removed.

Turn the oven temperature down to 140°c. Heat the coconut oil and sugar together in a saucepan over a medium heat until the sugar dissolves. Add all the remaining ingredients to the pan, including the roasted hazelnuts, and mix well to form a dough.

Place a rectangle of greaseproof paper on a baking tray. Place your biscuit dough on top and form it into a loaf, similar in shape and size to a ciabatta. Bake the loaf in the oven for about 30 minutes, until crisp on the outside. Cook for longer if necessary.

Remove the biscotti loaf from the oven and allow to cool completely before cutting into thick slices. I have found that a sharp bread knife works best in this situation. If you want a softer biscuit texture, you can eat them now. To make more traditional biscotti, bake the slices on the tray in the oven for about 10 minutes and then set aside on a wire rack to cool before serving.

COCONUT CARDAMOM PANNA COTTA WITH CINNAMON PLUMS

Preparation time: 15 minutes,
plus 2 hours setting
Cooking time: 15 minutes
Serves 4
Gluten-free

A little tip for making coconut cream is to refrigerate good quality coconut milk in a Pyrex jug overnight. The cream will rise to the surface and set so you can easily scoop it off, discarding the watery part underneath. Alternatively, you can buy good quality coconut cream in Asian supermarkets.

565ml coconut cream

190ml coconut milk

75g white sugar

20 cardamom pods, slightly cracked with the back of a knife

1 teaspoon vanilla paste

2.5g agar powder

4 ripe plums, quartered and destoned

2 teaspoons white sugar

1/2 teaspoon ground cinnamon

Combine the coconut cream, milk, sugar, cracked cardamom pods and vanilla in a saucepan. Meanwhile, weigh the agar powder as accurately as possible to ensure your panna cotta has the right texture. Too much will make it too firm, but too little will mean it won't set properly. Sprinkle the agar on top of the coconut mixture and let it sit for 10 minutes.

After 10 minutes, give the mixture a quick whisk to stir in the agar powder. Now bring it to the boil, stirring continuously. Keep this going for another 2 to 3 minutes to allow the agar and sugar to dissolve. The mixture should start to thicken at this point. Remove all the cardamom pods.

Transfer the panna cotta mixture into a jug and leave to cool for 5 minutes before pouring carefully and evenly into 4 moulds or some nice glasses. Panna cotta moulds are cheap and easy to use.

Transfer the panna cotta to the fridge to set and leave them for a couple of hours. About 10 minutes before you are ready to serve the panna cotta, place the quartered plums into a warm pan with the sugar and cinnamon to sear gently until they soften slightly. Serve alongside the panna cotta.

RAW RASPBERRY CHEESECAKE

Preparation time: 15 minutes, plus soaking
overnight and 8-12 hours setting
Serves 8-12
Gluten-free

A delicious, rich, indulgent cheesecake that is good for you.
What's not to love?

For the base

250g almonds

100g raisins

35g desiccated coconut

2 teaspoons vanilla paste

For the topping

450g frozen raspberries, thawed (fresh
is fine too)

400g cashews, soaked in water
overnight

125g lemon juice

125ml agave syrup

50ml maple syrup

1 teaspoon vanilla paste

175g coconut oil, melted

To serve

Fresh raspberries

Icing sugar (optional)

For the base

Place the almonds into a food processor and blend until they are the
consistency of flour. Next, add the raisins and blend until they are broken
down and incorporated into the almond flour. Add the coconut and vanilla
and blend until well mixed. You may need to add a teaspoon or two of water
to help the base stick together.

Press the mixture evenly into the bottom of a 9 inch/23cm springform cake
tin. Alternatively, you could line 8 to 12 small metal rings with high sides to
make individual cheesecakes.

For the topping

Make sure the raspberries are fully defrosted if you are using frozen, then
drain the soaked cashews and put them both in a high-speed blender with
all the other topping ingredients except the coconut oil. Blend until the
mixture is very smooth. You may need to scrape the sides down with a
spatula. Add the melted coconut oil and blend again until incorporated.

Pour the topping over the base and chill the cheesecake in the fridge for 8
to 12 hours. To serve, top the set cheesecake with fresh raspberries. Dust
with icing sugar if you want it to look pretty and you are not so concerned
about it being 100% raw.

STICKY TOFFEE PUDDING

Preparation time: 20 minutes
Cooking time: 1 hour
Serves 9

A classic British pudding that needs no introduction. We have veganised it here.

For the cake

180g dates

150ml water

375ml soya milk

190g margarine

150g soft brown sugar

2 tablespoons black treacle

350g self-raising white flour

1$^{1}/_{2}$ teaspoons bicarbonate of soda

1 teaspoon ground cinnamon

1 teaspoon ground ginger

$^{1}/_{2}$ teaspoon nutmeg

For the sauce

125g margarine

90g brown sugar

60ml maple syrup

1 teaspoon vanilla bean paste

65g soya cream

For the cake

Preheat your oven to 175°c and grease a 9 inch/23cm square cake tin with oil, then line it with greaseproof paper.

Chop the dates into small chunks and place them in a saucepan, cover with the water and soya milk, then simmer for 5 minutes until the dates are soft. Leave to cool in the fridge.

In a large bowl, beat the margarine and sugar together until pale and creamy. Add the cooled date mixture, black treacle, flour, bicarbonate of soda and spices to the bowl. Whisk it all together and give it a good beating.

Pour the cake mixture into the prepared tin and bake in the middle of the preheated oven for 40 minutes. Towards the end of the cooking time, check whether the cake is cooked right through by poking a fine knife or skewer into the centre. It should come out clean when the cake is ready.

For the sauce

While the cake is baking, make your sticky toffee sauce. Place all the ingredients except the cream in a medium saucepan and bring to a gentle simmer. Cook the sauce until it begins to thicken, then take the pan off the heat and whisk in the cream until evenly combined.

To serve

Leaving it in the tin, cut the cake into 3 inch squares. Pour some of the toffee sauce over the top while both the cake and the sauce are still hot, so it partly soaks in and forms a glaze. Serve the sticky toffee pudding with your favourite non-dairy ice cream and extra sauce in a jug on the table.

Sauces, Chutneys & Dips

APRICOT CHUTNEY

Preparation time: 15 minutes
Cooking time: 1 hour
Makes about 1 litre
Gluten-free

This easy apricot chutney is just a slight variation on mango chutney for something different. It goes really well with the korma on page 90.

250g dried apricots

750ml water

125ml white wine vinegar

25g fresh ginger, minced

1 small onion, finely diced

4 cardamom pods

2 star anise

2 tablespoons white sugar

1 tablespoon brown sugar

1 teaspoon salt

Chop the apricots in a food processor or by hand with a sharp knife. Put all the remaining ingredients into a pan and bring to the boil. Once boiling, add the apricots and then gently simmer for an hour or so, stirring every now and again to avoid anything sticking to the bottom of the pan. Stir more frequently towards the end as the chutney reduces. It will keep for a month in a sterilised airtight container and freezes well.

COCONUT CHUTNEY

Preparation time: 10 minutes
Cooking time: 5 minutes
Makes approx. 300ml
Gluten-free

This great South Indian chutney goes with many Indian snacks, such as the potato bonda on page 58. Make sure you buy coconut meat, which you can often find frozen in Asian food shops. Using desiccated coconut will not work here as it will be very chewy. Alternatively, you could grate the white flesh of a whole fresh coconut. This chutney freezes well, so you could scale up the recipe and store in batches.

150g fresh coconut meat, grated

2 green chillies, deseeded and finely chopped

Thumb-sized piece of fresh ginger, peeled and grated

Salt, to taste

100ml water

For tempering the chutney

1 tablespoon coconut oil or sunflower oil

1 teaspoon mustard seeds

10 fresh curry leaves

1/2 teaspoon asafoetida (hing)

1 dried red chilli, deseeded and broken up

Put the grated coconut, chopped green chilli, grated ginger, salt and water into a blender and blitz until combined. If you prefer a thinner consistency, add a little more water here. I like it fairly thin so I can dip potato bonda into it.

For tempering the chutney

Heat the oil in a frying pan and then add the mustard seeds. Fry until they begin to pop, then add the curry leaves, asafoetida and dried red chilli. Fry for a few seconds until the curry leaves crisp up.

Add the hot spices and oil to the coconut mix and stir through. The chutney is now ready to serve.

BROWN SAUCE

Preparation time: 10 minutes
Cooking time: 45 minutes
Makes 1.5 litres
Gluten-free

This recipe makes a large batch to freeze in individual portions. Like the other sauces in this chapter, it's difficult to eat shop-bought brown sauce again after tasting the freshly made stuff!

50ml olive oil

500g onion, diced

150g celery, sliced

1/2 teaspoon chilli powder

1 teaspoon ground coriander

1 teaspoon allspice

3 cloves

1 x 400g tin of chopped tomatoes

130g dates

2 fresh bay leaves

80g white sugar

3 tablespoons tamarind paste

180ml white wine vinegar

200ml water

Salt and pepper

Gently heat the olive oil in a large saucepan, then add the onion and celery. Sauté them on a medium to high heat for 10 minutes, until nicely browned.

Stir in the spices and cook for a further 5 minutes. Add the tinned tomatoes, dates, bay leaves, sugar, half the tamarind paste, two thirds of the vinegar and all the water. Stir well and then simmer on a low heat until it reaches a sauce consistency (this should take roughly 30 minutes).

Purée the sauce in a food processor and then add the remaining tamarind and vinegar. Season with salt and pepper to taste. If needed, stir in a little more water at this stage to achieve your preferred consistency. Transfer the brown sauce to sterilised jars or individual containers to freeze.

CHILLI SAUCE WITH
LEMON AND OREGANO

Preparation time: 15 minutes
Makes 500ml
Gluten-free

This is similar to the Portuguese piri piri sauce. I recommend using this recipe as a guide and experimenting with different ingredients such as basil, smoked paprika or hotter chillies.

10 long red chillies

150ml lemon juice

150ml olive oil

35g good quality paprika

35g soft brown sugar

10g fresh oregano leaves

10g black pepper

5g salt

Halve the chillies lengthways and deseed them. Place in a blender with the remaining ingredients and blend until very smooth. This sauce will keep in a sterilised jar in the fridge for a few weeks.

FERMENTED SRIRACHA HOT SAUCE

Preparation time: 3-5 days

Cooking time: 5-10 minutes

Makes 500ml

Gluten-free

This is a traditional Thai chilli sauce that should be sweet, spicy, garlicky and tangy. Do not substitute the distilled white vinegar, as the recipe won't work with other varieties.

250g red Thai chillies (the short fat ones, not bird's eye)

125g long red chillies

5 cloves of garlic, peeled

1 tablespoon sea salt

1 tablespoon light brown sugar

1 teaspoon white sugar

100ml water

120ml distilled white vinegar

Cut all the chillies in half lengthways and scrape out the seeds with the back of your knife. Place the chillies and seeds in a powerful blender with the garlic, salt, sugars and water. Blend until smooth.

Transfer the blended mixture into a large sterilised glass jar, cover with cling film and then leave in a cool dark place for 3 to 5 days, stirring once a day. The chilli mixture will start to bubble and ferment. You may need to scrape down the sides during this process. It is very important to stir it every day.

After the fermentation period has finished, return the fermented chilli mixture to the blender along with the distilled white vinegar and blend until smooth. Strain the liquid through a fine sieve into a saucepan and push as much of the pulp through the sieve as you can. Discard the remaining seeds and skin left in the sieve.

Heat the sauce on a medium heat for 5 to 10 minutes and reduce until it reaches your desired thickness. Transfer your sauce to sterilised bottles and enjoy with everything!

MOSCOW MULE CHILLI SAUCE

Preparation time: 15 minutes
Cooking time: 30 minutes
Makes 1 litre
Gluten-free

A Moscow Mule is a cocktail, but we have taken some of the key ingredients (vodka, ginger beer, lime juice) and turned them into a delicious and unusual chilli sauce. It should keep in the fridge for weeks in an airtight sterilised bottle or jar.

150g red or green chillies, deseeded

150g brown sugar

400ml white wine vinegar

100ml lime juice

50ml vodka

4 cloves of garlic

150ml olive oil

300ml ginger beer

A few fresh mint leaves

In a medium saucepan, combine the chillies, sugar, vinegar, lime juice and vodka. Bring the mixture to the boil, then reduce the heat and gently simmer for 20 minutes. You will probably want your extractor fan on, or a window open here.

Remove 50ml of the cooking liquor from the pan and set aside. Transfer the chillies into a blender, add the peeled garlic cloves and blitz until smooth.

Heat a little of the olive oil in a clean pan and then fry the garlic and chilli pulp for 1 minute. Now add the remaining olive oil, ginger beer and 50ml of reserved cooking liquor.

Leave the sauce to simmer until it reaches your preferred thickness. Leave it to cool before adding the fresh mint and blending once more.

MUSTARD AND HERB CHILLI SAUCE

Preparation time: 10 minutes
Cooking time: less than 5 minutes
Makes approx. 1 litre
Gluten-free

A lot of the ingredients in this recipe are interchangeable. Use whichever chillies you like, choosing a variety that suits your preferences for flavour and heat. Pick whatever soft herbs you like too. Coriander is a good option with chilli.

150g green chillies

6 cloves of garlic

1 carrot

4 spring onions

10g fresh parsley

10g fresh chervil

10g fresh thyme leaves

200ml distilled white vinegar

200ml water

100g Dijon mustard

25g white sugar

1 tablespoon fine sea salt

1/2 teaspoon white pepper

First, prepare the chillies by removing their stems, halving them lengthways and deseeding them. Peel and slice the garlic, carrot and spring onions while you bring a pan of water to the boil.

Using a slotted spoon, blanch the chillies, garlic and carrot in the boiling water for 3 minutes before transferring to a blender. Next, blanch the fresh herbs for about 10 seconds before adding them to the blender with all the remaining ingredients.

Blend the mixture until very smooth, scraping the sides of the blender down if necessary. Transfer the sauce to sterilised airtight bottles or jars and refrigerate. It will last in the fridge for 3 months.

PEPPERCORN SAUCE

Preparation time: 5 minutes
Cooking time: 10 minutes
Makes 500ml
Gluten-free when using gluten-free gravy

1 shallot, finely diced

3/4 tablespoon coarsely ground black peppercorns

50ml brandy

250ml gravy (homemade or shop-bought)

150ml soya milk

5g arrowroot

2 tablespoons alternative cream

Salt, to taste

This sauce is usually served with beef but we have reinvented it to be served with our seitan steak. You can vary which peppercorns you use; pink peppercorns can add a little more delicacy to the flavour. You can substitute arrowroot with cornflour if needed; use slightly less if so.

Gently fry the shallot in a little oil with the black pepper. When the shallot is translucent, add the brandy and cook for a couple of minutes. Add the gravy and soya milk, then simmer for 5 minutes.

Mix the arrowroot to a paste with a little cold water, making sure there are no lumps. Stir this paste into the saucepan and cook for a few more minutes until the sauce has thickened. You can whisk gently here to check the consistency. Repeat the process with a little more arrowroot if the sauce is not thick enough. Stir in the cream, taste the sauce and season with salt.

PLUM KETCHUP

Preparation time: 10 minutes
Cooking time: 1 hour
Makes 1 litre
Gluten-free

500g ripe plums, destoned

1 medium onion, chopped

125ml red wine vinegar

70g brown sugar

70g white sugar

1 tin of plum tomatoes

1 teaspoon salt

1/2 teaspoon ground cinnamon

This recipe came about because we wanted something a little different than your bog-standard tomato ketchup, with a little more acidity and a flavour that was not going to overpower the rest of the dish.

Place all the ingredients in a heavy-bottomed saucepan and bring to the boil. Gently simmer with the lid on for a good hour before blending in a blender until smooth.

Taste the ketchup to check for sweetness, saltiness and sourness, then adjust the seasoning according to your preference. This can be frozen.

TOMATO CHUTNEY

Preparation time: 10 minutes, plus 20 minutes to cool
Cooking time: 20 minutes
Serves 10
Gluten-free

1 teaspoon cumin seeds

3 dried red chillies

1 small red onion, diced

4cm piece of fresh ginger, grated

4 cloves of garlic, finely chopped

6 medium-size tomatoes, chopped

2 fresh curry leaves

1 teaspoon salt

Pinch of ground turmeric

A nice and spicy semi-authentic Indian chutney; I took out some of the faffier processes that don't add much to the finished product, which also reduced the cooking time. The tomatoes need to be really ripe and full of flavour for best results.

Heat a tablespoon of oil in a pan, then add the cumin seeds and fry for 1 minute. Now add the dried chillies, onion, ginger and garlic and fry on a medium heat for 5 minutes until the onion turns golden. Stir in the chopped tomatoes, curry leaves, salt and turmeric. Sauté until the mixture is soft and mushy and the raw smell of tomatoes has disappeared. Allow the chutney to cool, then blend until smooth.

TAHINI SAUCE

Preparation time: 10 minutes
Makes 500ml
Gluten-free

I think I could eat anything covered in enough tahini sauce! This recipe is a traditional one from the Middle East.

50ml lemon juice

25ml olive oil

2 cloves of garlic (not too big)

150g tahini

175ml water

Salt, to taste

Blend the lemon juice, olive oil and garlic in a food processor until the garlic is puréed. Add the tahini and water, blend again, then taste and season with salt. Serve at room temperature.

TAMARIND SAUCE

Preparation time: 5 minutes
Cooking time: 5 minutes
Makes 300ml
Gluten-free

I have used tamarind concentrate in this recipe because it's available in most supermarkets, but normally you would use pulp or the whole fruit. If you are fortunate enough to live near an Indian or Thai market then use three times the amount of dried tamarind fruit with the stones removed instead of the concentrate.

250ml water

100g white sugar

40g tamarind concentrate

1 teaspoon black salt

1 teaspoon sea salt

1 teaspoon black pepper

1/2 teaspoon ground ginger

Good pinch of chilli powder (optional)

Place all the ingredients in a pan and boil gently for 5 minutes. If you used dried tamarind fruit instead of concentrate, then you will need to blend the sauce for a smooth consistency.

TOMATO KETCHUP

Preparation time: 10 minutes
Cooking time: 1 hour 30 minutes
Makes approx. 1 litre
Gluten-free

This is another one of those recipes that means you will find it hard to eat the nutritionally bankrupt shop-bought variety after making your own. It makes a large quantity that can be frozen in portions and defrosted for use as needed.

1 large onion, roughly chopped

1 clove of garlic, roughly chopped

1 teaspoon ground fennel

1 teaspoon celery salt

1 teaspoon paprika

Olive oil

1 x 400g tin of chopped tomatoes

1 tablespoon tomato purée

2 tablespoons white sugar

100ml apple juice

60ml red wine vinegar

Gently cook the onion, garlic and seasonings in a little oil on a low to medium heat until the onion is soft and translucent (this should take about 15 minutes). Next, add the tomatoes, purée, sugar, apple juice and half of the vinegar. Simmer on a low heat for 1 hour.

Remove the pan from the heat and pour the ketchup into a blender. Season well with salt and pepper, then blend until smooth.

Once cooled, stir in the remaining vinegar and taste. If you prefer your ketchup slightly sweeter, leave it as it is, or add a little more vinegar if you prefer a tarter flavour. Decant into sterilised jars or plastic tubs if you want to freeze the ketchup.

TURMERIC AND GINGER KIMCHI

Preparation time: 20 minutes, plus 2 days
fermentation
Makes approx. 2kg
Gluten-free

Kimchi is a traditional Korean pickle eaten with nearly every meal. We love it so much that we wanted to eat it with a creamy curry, so we messed around with the recipe by adding fresh turmeric, ginger and mustard seeds to give it a more Indian flavour.

1 Chinese leaf cabbage

6 tablespoons fine sea salt

1kg carrots, peeled and cut into matchsticks

2 daikon radishes, peeled and cut into matchsticks

3 bunches of spring onions, washed and sliced

15cm fresh turmeric, finely grated

2 tablespoons finely grated ginger

2 tablespoons gochujang paste

3 tablespoons mustard seeds

Wash and slice the Chinese cabbage, then place in a colander and cover evenly with the salt. Leave for 2 hours, turning and massaging the cabbage every 30 minutes so it salts evenly. After 2 hours, rinse off any excess salt from the cabbage and place in a large bowl.

Add all the remaining ingredients to the bowl and toss everything together with clean hands. Leave the bowl at room temperature for an hour or so to soften the vegetables.

Fill an airtight container with the kimchi mixture and push down to break up the vegetables so they release their juices. Make sure you pack the container tightly so no air can get inside and seal it with the lid.

Leave the kimchi at room temperature for 2 days to ferment before using. Once ready, store in the refrigerator where it will keep for a long time.

VEGAN MAYONNAISE

Preparation time: 10 minutes, plus 30-40 minutes cooling
Cooking time: 10 minutes
Makes 1 litre
Gluten-free

This recipe makes a really good mayonnaise that does not split. You could add a few cloves of garlic or some chipotle powder for extra flavour if you like. It tastes even better liberally applied to chips!

450g cold water

100g chickpea flour, sifted

1 teaspoon salt

1/2 tsp Dijon mustard (optional)

25ml lemon juice

60ml white wine vinegar

300ml rapeseed oil

Add the water, chickpea flour and salt to a saucepan and whisk to combine. Bring to a gentle boil and whisk constantly until the mixture starts to thicken, then remove from the heat and continue to whisk before pouring it straight into a plastic tray or a baking tray lined with greaseproof paper. Allow to cool a little before refrigerating.

When the flour mixture has cooled and set, break it up into pieces and place in a blender. Add the mustard, lemon juice and white wine vinegar and blend to combine. With the blender running, add the rapeseed oil in a trickle, slowly pouring so the mayonnaise emulsifies. If you add all the oil in one go, it will split.

QUICK VEGAN MAYONNAISE

Preparation time: 5 minutes
Makes 500ml
Gluten-free

This is an even quicker and easier alternative to the above. Adding a little sugar softens the edges of the vinegar but is optional.

375g silken tofu

45ml white wine vinegar

1 teaspoon salt

1/2 teaspoon white sugar (optional)

1/2 teaspoon Dijon mustard

6 tablespoons rapeseed oil

Place all the ingredients except the rapeseed oil in a blender and blend until the mixture is smooth. Slowly add the oil in a thin stream while the blender is running until it is incorporated.

Basics

CHAAT MASALA

Preparation time: 5 minutes
Cooking time: 10 minutes
Makes 1 small jar
Gluten-free

This is a ubiquitous Indian finishing spice blend. Sprinkle it over freshly cooked samosas, pakoras or even a very simple salad.

3 tablespoons cumin seeds

1 tablespoon coriander seeds

1 tablespoon black peppercorns

4 tablespoons dried mango powder (amchoor)

3 tablespoons black salt

2 teaspoons ajwain seeds

1 teaspoon ground ginger

1/2 teaspoon asafoetida (hing)

Dry fry the cumin seeds, coriander seeds and black peppercorns on a low heat until they become fragrant. This will take about 7 minutes. Allow to cool.

Add the cooled seeds and peppercorns to the rest of the ingredients and then grind them to a powder in either a pestle and mortar or a spice grinder. Store the chaat masala in an airtight container.

GARLIC AND GINGER PASTE

Preparation time: 10 minutes
Makes 400g
Gluten-free

This paste is used in nearly every curry and it's always good to keep some in the fridge. It can also be used to freshen up a pre-made curry by quickly frying a spoonful before stirring it into the sauce.

200g peeled ginger

200g peeled garlic

Chop the ginger and garlic into more manageable pieces, then place them in the food processor and blitz to a paste. You can add a little water here to help it along if needed.

I quite often blend the paste as finely as possible before transferring it to a container and topping it with a thin layer of neutral oil. It will keep in the fridge like this for 1 month and can also be frozen in portions for future use.

CHOLE MASALA

Preparation time: 10 minutes
Cooking time: 5 minutes
Makes 1 medium jar
Gluten-free

Whole Spices

12 dried Kashmiri chillies, halved lengthways and stems removed

1 cinnamon stick

1 teaspoon cardamom seeds

1 teaspoon cloves

4 dried bay leaves

4 tablespoons coriander seeds

2 tablespoons cumin seeds

2 tablespoons pomegranate seeds

2 teaspoons black peppercorns

2 teaspoons ajwain seeds

1 teaspoon fennel seeds

Ground Spices

3 teaspoons black salt

2 teaspoons dried mango powder (amchoor)

1 teaspoon ground nutmeg

1 teaspoon ground ginger

1/2 teaspoon ground mace

1/2 teaspoon asafoetida (hing)

This chickpea spice blend is hard to beat, and it definitely tastes much better made at home rather than purchased from a shop. The recipe below is just a rough guide, so play around with the quantities and add a little more of the spices you love.

You will need 2 separate pans for this recipe. In the first pan, dry fry the Kashmiri chillies, cinnamon stick, cardamom seeds, cloves and bay leaves on a gentle heat for about 5 minutes, or until they start to become fragrant.

In your other pan, dry fry the remaining whole spices on a low to medium heat until fragrant. Allow both lots of spices to cool before combining them all with the ground spices.

Blend the mixture in a spice grinder or a regular blender to form a powder. Store the chole masala in an airtight container for up to 3 months.

COCONUT BACON

Preparation time: 10-15 minutes
Cooking time: 15-30 minutes
Makes 75g
Gluten-free

75g flaked coconut

2 tablespoons tamari

1 tablespoon maple syrup

1 tablespoon oil

1 teaspoon smoked paprika

1/2 teaspoon liquid smoke

Fine sea salt, to taste

This is a simple recipe for a tasty addition to salads. It's also great when broken up a bit and sprinkled into a creamy pasta sauce.

Preheat your oven to 140°c. Mix all the ingredients together and leave the mixture to stand for 10 minutes or so, then spread it out on a non-stick baking tray.

Bake the marinated coconut in the preheated oven for 6 minutes and then remove from the oven and stir. Bake for another 6 minutes, check again, then repeat this process until you achieve a dark golden colour. The 'bacon' needs to be cooked low and slow, as you do not want the coconut to blacken. You are aiming for the pieces to be dried out and the right colour, but no more than that.

Keep checking the tray, especially towards the end of the cooking time, because the coconut bacon can go from cooked to burnt quite quickly. When done, remove from the oven and leave to cool.

DEMI-GLACE

Preparation time: 20 minutes

Cooking time: 1 hour 30 minutes

Makes a large batch

Gluten-free when using gluten-free yeast extract

500g mushrooms

1 leek

1 carrot

4 large shallots

4 cloves of garlic

Olive oil

75g tomato purée

50g yeast extract

500ml red wine

500ml Port

200ml tamari

1 litre homemade stock

50g dried mushrooms

2 bay leaves

This rich sauce is a great thing to keep in your freezer; a spoonful or two can really give certain dishes great depth of flavour. You can even add some water or stock and some arrowroot or cornflour to the finished sauce for a great gravy.

Roughly chop the mushrooms, wash and slice the leek and carrot, then peel and slice the shallots and garlic. Meanwhile, heat a little oil in a large, heavy-bottomed pan. Fry all the prepared vegetables except the garlic until they are browning and all of the liquid has evaporated, then add the garlic and cook for another 2 minutes.

Stir in the tomato purée and yeast extract, then cook for another 3 minutes. Add the wine and Port, then cook for another 5 minutes until the alcohol has evaporated.

Add the tamari, stock, dried mushrooms and bay leaves, then leave to cook for 30 minutes. After this time, turn off the heat and leave to stand for another 20 minutes.

Strain the liquid through a fine mesh sieve into a clean pan. Press the vegetables with the back of a wooden spoon to extract all the juices, then discard the solids.

Place the pan of liquid back on the heat and reduce for 30 minutes until you have a rich sauce. This recipe makes a fairly sizeable batch so once cooled, freeze the demi-glace in individual portions.

GARLIC AND PARSLEY OIL

Preparation time: 5 minutes

Makes approx. 500ml

Gluten-free

500ml olive oil

5 cloves of garlic

30g fresh flat leaf parsley leaves

This is good to keep a stock of in the fridge as it lasts well. Use it in a variety of ways such as dressing vegetables, frying greens or as a base for a salad dressing.

Add all the ingredients to a blender and blend well. Store in sterilised glass jars in the fridge.

BASIC VEGETABLE STOCK

Preparation time: 10 minutes
Cooking time: 45 minutes
Makes approx. 2 litres
Gluten-free

3 carrots, including tops

3 onions, including skins

9 sticks of celery, including leaves

1 tomato

4 fresh bay leaves

2 tablespoons black peppercorns

2.5 litres water

A flavourful stock can transform a good dish into a great one. On the flip side, there's nothing wrong with a good quality stock cube thrown into the mix at an appropriate time. Making your own is a great way to use up vegetable odds and ends though.

Save all your carrot tops, celery leaves and onion skins in an airtight container in the fridge for up to a week to make this stock with. 99% of the time our stocks are made from vegetable odds and ends, but don't use anything that has too much colour (such as beetroot) or anything starchy. We don't put garlic in either because the sugars turn bitter easily. A great piece of advice I was given as a young chef was: "don't include anything you wouldn't eat; a stock pot is not a rubbish bin." Whatever you're using, make sure all your vegetables are clean before chopping them very roughly.

Put all the ingredients into a large pot so the water comes to about 5cm above the vegetables, then simmer really gently for about 40 minutes. If you cook the stock for too much longer than an hour, the flavour will turn bitter. Strain the stock through a fine sieve to remove any debris and discard the solids. Allow to cool if you are storing the stock, but it is always best used fresh.

CHINESE VEGETABLE STOCK

Preparation time: 10 minutes
Cooking time: 40 minutes
Makes 2.5 litres
Gluten-free

30ml vegetable cooking oil

1 daikon radish, peeled and cubed

1 carrot, peeled and cubed

2 onions, peeled and halved

4 celery sticks, cut into sections

50g fresh mushrooms

3 litres water

8 dried mushrooms

2 teaspoons salt

Pinch of black pepper

This lively yet simple stock brings depth of flavour to many dishes. I got the recipe on a trip to Hong Kong. Splash in a little of this stock when cooking stir fries to partially steam the vegetables instead of using too much oil.

Heat the cooking oil in a large pot before adding all the vegetables and fresh mushrooms. Stir fry the vegetables and mushrooms for about 5 to 7 minutes until lightly browned.

Add the water, dried mushrooms, salt and black pepper to the pot. When the water comes to a boil, turn the heat down and simmer gently for 30 minutes.

Strain the soup stock and discard the vegetables. If you don't need it all straight away, freeze the remainder in portions to use as required.

MASALA GRAVY

Preparation time: 15 minutes
Cooking time: 1 hour 30 minutes
Makes 12 portions
Gluten-free

I spent three years managing a small chain of Indian restaurants in New Zealand, and during the daytime I would go in and hang out with the Indian and Nepalese chefs to help prep, trying to pick up tips and techniques for closely guarded recipes. This masala gravy (or a variation of it) is used as a base in nearly all restaurant-style curries, especially here in the UK. It gives a lovely thick sweet sauce to any curry.

1.5kg white onions, peeled and chopped

200g carrots, peeled and chopped

150g white cabbage, chopped

1 red pepper, deseeded and chopped

1 green pepper, deseeded and chopped

1 tin of chopped tomatoes

6 tablespoons puréed garlic

6 tablespoons puréed ginger

500ml rapeseed oil

2 tablespoons ground coriander

2 tablespoons ground cumin

2 tablespoons paprika (good quality)

2 tablespoons garam masala

1 tablespoon turmeric

This recipe makes enough for 12 portions that you can freeze in individual containers and pull out a couple of hours before making your favourite curry. If you do not have a large enough pot to cook it in, just halve the recipe.

Place all the chopped vegetables, tinned tomatoes and purées into a large pan. Pour in the oil along with about 750ml of water. It may seem like a lot of oil, but it is skimmed off later.

Bring the mixture to the boil over a medium heat, then reduce to a simmer and cook with a lid on for about 40 minutes. Now add another 2 litres of water, stir in all the spices and continue to simmer for another 30 minutes. After this time, the oil should rise to the top and everything in the pan should be soft. Now let it sit so the flavoured oil on top can all be skimmed off with a ladle and stored in a clean container. Use this to fry your curry sauce ingredients or just use a few drops to finish a dish.

The gravy is now ready to blend, either with a stick blender or in a jug blender. Blend until the liquid is really smooth with no bits. It should be fairly thin but will reduce when you are cooking your curry. It will taste like a weak curried onion gravy.

GLOSSARY

Agar Agar

A seaweed extract which works similarly to gelatine. It comes in flakes or powder but we find powder works best.

Agave Syrup

The sweet syrup of the agave family of plants, originating from Mexico. It is sweet and does not have a lot of flavour but a good swap if you avoid refined sugar.

Amchoor

Also known as amchur, this is a dried powder made from green unripe mangoes. It has a citrus flavour similar to citric acid.

Arrowroot

A powder made from dried root shoots of several tropical plants. It can be used as a thickener and works well because it is clear when thick.

Banana Blossom

This is the teardrop shaped fleshy flower at the bottom of a cluster of bananas. It can be eaten raw and its flaky texture makes it ideal as a fish substitute.

Black Salt

Also known as kala namak, this salt is more pink than black and used a lot in Indian cuisine. It has a sulphurous smell and taste not too unlike eggs, ideal for scrambled tofu.

Daikon Radish

Also known as mooli, a long white radish from Southeast Asia.

Demi-glace

A French rich brown sauce, strong in flavour, traditionally made with roasted beef bone stock.

Egg Replacer

We used the Crack'D brand to replicate eggs in baking.

Exotic Mushrooms

Varieties include oyster, chanterelle, lion's mane, shiitake, black and yellow trumpet and shimeji.

Fava Beans

Dried broad beans that originate from the Middle East.

Fenugreek

This is an annual plant from the Indian subcontinent. The leaves and seeds are used in cooking and have been since ancient times.

Gluten Flour

Sometimes called vital wheat gluten. It is a flour-like powder which is nearly all protein and very little starch. Often used to make seitan and a handy ingredient to add when baking bread, especially when the bread has lots of added ingredients such as nuts and seeds.

Miso

A traditional Japanese seasoning, usually in paste form. It is made by fermenting soya beans with koji and salt as well as ingredients such as seaweed, rice and barley. It is a rich paste with a great umami flavour.

Nori

This is a dried edible seaweed used in Japanese cooking. It is often used to wrap sushi.

Nutritional Yeast

This is a deactivated yeast in the form of yellow flakes. It has a cheesy, nutty flavour.

Quinoa

This is a flowering plant in the amaranth family. The seeds are used in cooking. They are rich in protein, fibre and B vitamins.

Rejuvelac

A type of grain water and a fermented drink rich in prebiotics.

Silken Tofu

Much softer and creamier than regular tofu. It has a much higher water content than normal varieties (80% as opposed to about 50%). It looks and feels more like a firm yoghurt.

Tamari

A Japanese version of soy sauce. No wheat is used in the process of making tamari so it is gluten-free. It tends to be richer and slightly less salty than soy sauce. If you are swapping soy sauce for tamari then use a little less.

Tamarind

An edible fruit that grows on the tamarind tree. The tree produces brown pod-like fruits that contain a sweet tangy pulp used in cooking.

Tempeh

Indonesian fermented soya beans that bind together during the fermentation process. It is rich in highly digestible protein.

The Green Rock